ARMS AND ARMOUR OF
THE RENAISSANCE JOUST

Tobias Capwell

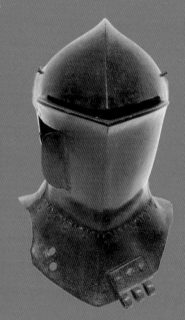

CONTENTS

Front cover: Garniture of Sir Robert
Dudley, Earl of Leicester, by John
Kelte, Greenwich, *c.*1575. II.81

Page 1: Great bascinet for the
joust, Italian, *c.*1500. AL.31

INTRODUCTION

This book continues the story begun in Arms and Armour of the Medieval Joust, which traced the history of jousting through the collection of the Royal Armouries, from its origins in the twelfth century up to the end of the fifteenth century. Here we begin in 1500, and will follow the story to its end in the seventeenth century.

The joust first appeared in the twelfth century, as a preamble to the mass combat of the tournament. By the fourteenth century however, it had replaced the tourney as the most prestigious form of knightly combat. It diversified into several different forms – jousts of war, run in the same gear used on the battlefield, and jousts of peace, employing specially-designed safety equipment. By the fifteenth century the different joust forms had developed quite specific emphases. Some were primarily demonstrations of skill, while others promoted feats of strength or superlative horsemanship. All, however, represented a kind of archetypal confrontation between two elemental forces. The expressive or dramatic potential of the joust is the key to understanding its later history.

The Renaissance is best known for its famous artists, but it is also the story of the noblemen who challenged painters and sculptors to create great art. The patrons of Michelangelo, da Vinci, Titian, and Holbein were also knights and jousters. As such, they also played a central role in another great Renaissance art-form, that of the armourer. The European aristocracy needed armour for war but also, by the late fifteenth century, for grand spectacles enacting mythic and allegorical fantasies. The jousts of the Renaissance developed knightly combat into performance art celebrating the divine and supernatural forces which determined the order of the earthly realm. The settings were legendary, but the combats were real. The joust was both a physical and conceptual collision – of the two participants, and of fantasy and reality. Superhuman feats occurred before the eyes of the audience, deeds made possible by the skill of the combatants and the properties of their equipment. The Renaissance joust quickly became a political tool and a social phenomenon. Its potential was seized by a new generation of Renaissance princes striving to uphold the chivalric tradition whilst also embracing new technologies and military practices. From 1500 onwards, the joust was defined more than ever before by the agendas of particular rulers, men who drove their courtly culture with force of personality and personal physical prowess, proving their rights on the bodies of their opponents.

Tobias Capwell
Curator of Arms and Armour, The Wallace Collection

THE LAST KNIGHT

▲ The Emperor Maximilian I, by Bernhard Striegel, after 1508. © Tiroler Landsmuseum Ferdinandeum Innsbruck

One of the most important people in the history of jousting is Holy Roman Emperor Maximilian I (1459–1519), ruler of the German Lands. Maximilian laid the foundations for the vibrant jousting culture which thrived throughout most of the sixteenth century and in many ways, his reign forms a bridge between the Middle Ages and the Renaissance. Indeed, Maximilian went to great lengths to portray himself as a kind of fusion of two identities – of the ideal medieval king and the enlightened Renaissance prince. In battle he fought in the front ranks alongside his men according to the old tradition, but famously as a pikeman deployed on foot, not always as a heavy cavalryman. He dedicated himself to excellence in the fighting arts of the medieval knight, with sword, spear, axe and dagger, while also promoting diverse new forms of combat, including the mastery of firearms and artillery. Maximilian's image of the strong ruler drew legitimacy from the past and relevance from the present, creating an identity of unique power. Contemporaries and successors took much from the example of a man who is still called 'The Last Knight'.

JOUSTING MANIA AT THE IMPERIAL COURT OF MAXIMILIAN

▲ 'How the White King gained expertise in the fabrication of armour', from *Der Weisskunig* (1514–16).

At the zenith of the German Renaissance, jousting played a crucial role in a wider chivalric revival promoted by Maximilian. Under his patronage, three semi-fictional biographies were written about him, all in the style of chivalric romance. *Der Weisskunig*, *Freydal*, and *Theuerdank* cast the Emperor as a heroic knight, the embodiment of a romantic tradition, who led every aspect of his life according to the ancient ideals of chivalry.

For Maximilian therefore, the joust was of fundamental importance. It prepared the just ruler for war while also demonstrating formidable battle-readiness to the world in a setting of utter magnificence. Maximilian claimed to have rejuvenated the armourer's art in Germany, and certainly under his patronage it flourished. Two of the greatest armourers who ever lived, Lorenz Helmschmid of Augsburg and Konrad Seusenhofer of Innsbruck (where Maximilian established his court armoury in 1504) devised new types of jousting armour for him. Their efforts, in close personal collaboration with the Emperor, produced a diversity of new joust forms, each of which required its own unique equipment. Maximilian's lead in jousting fashion was then followed at Ducal and Electoral courts throughout the Empire.

The various jousting styles practiced at the Imperial court fall into two main typologies: *Stechen* and *Rennen*. These classifications were nostalgically portrayed as the traditional jousts of peace and war respectively, but these distinctions, in the context of Habsburg court spectacles, are somewhat misleading. True jousts of war continued to be practiced into the second half of the sixteenth century, and their definition for purposes here remains the same – they were encounters run in the real equipment of the battlefield, with very little (if any) special modifications. None of the elaborate jousts fashionable at the court of Maximilian can strictly be described as 'true' jousts of war, since they were all run in specially-designed sports equipment of one sort or another. The jousts known collectively as *Rennen* were by this period all 'mock' jousts of war.

▲ A foreign joust of peace (Welsches Gestech), preparatory sketch for *Freydal*, *c*.1512–15.
© National Gallery of Art, Washington

This should not however be taken to mean that Maximilian's courses were somehow softer or safer than those practiced in the Middle Ages. Indeed, these were some of the roughest versions of

▲ Rider armed for the Anzogen Rennen, South German, *c*.1500. © Akademie der bildenden Künste, Kupferstichkabinett, Vienna

the game ever played. They were perhaps less explicitly dangerous than genuine jousts of war, but certainly they involved much harder hits than anything experienced by any medieval jouster. Lances grew to monstrous proportions; some of the new German types could reach diameters of as much as five inches along most of their length. To support these enormous weapons, an additional rear lance support, the *queue*, was fitted to some types of jousting harness. Blows delivered in the heaviest German jousts were truly massive: riders could be ripped forcibly out of the saddle, while horse and man could be thrown together to the ground. Maximilian's jousts most often required the riders to use flat-backed saddles, making it even more difficult to retain one's seat whilst dealing and receiving heavy blows.

All *Stechen* practiced in the time of Maximilian were straightforward jousts of peace, employing coronels, frog-mouthed helms, and other obviously non-military pieces of equipment. The emphasis, certainly in the most distinctively German form (*Deutsches Gestech*), was strength above all else. The armour (*Stechzeug*) was very strongly-built and heavy, as were the lances and horses used. Unsurprisingly, the speeds at which these courses were run were rather slower than most other jousts. This meant that when the lance struck the opponent, it remained in contact with him for a greater amount of time, producing a pushing action which lasted until the lance broke, one or both jousters fell, or a horse was thrown to the ground. Sometimes, all of those results occurred at the same

▲ Composite armour for the German joust of peace *(Deutsches Gestech)*, Nuremberg and Augsburg, *c.*1510–30. © The Wallace Collection, London

◀ The German joust of peace (Deutsches Gestech), from *Freydal*, Vienna, *c.*1512–15. © KHM, Vienna

time. This slower tempo and the quality of the action it produced may be the origin of the term Stechen ('sticking', 'stabbing' or 'prodding'). The term might also allude to the fact that all Stechen employed multipointed coronels, rather than single points, which were designed to bite or stick into the wooden shield, or otherwise gain purchase on the opponent's armour, without piercing it.

However, even within one joust-form typology, the physical emphasis could vary quite significantly. German jousts of peace still did not employ the tilt, almost a hundred years after it was introduced in western Europe. Three of the four Stechen forms practiced at the court of Maximilian, the German Gestech, the Gestech in high saddles (*Hohenzeug Gestech*), and the Gestech in leg armour (*Gestech im Beinharnisch*), were all run 'at random', that is, in the open field. The tilt was regarded as a foreign affectation, and only used in one course, of all the many imperial forms. The 'foreign' Gestech

▲ Lance-head for the Stechen, German, *c.*1500–20. © Metropolitan Museum of Art, New York

(*Welsches Gestech*), as its name implies, is the German iteration of the standard joust of peace or 'joust royal' practiced throughout the rest of Europe. Although it still employed jousting armour which was somewhat heavier than war armour, the 'foreign' Gestech was, overall, a lighter and faster version of the joust of peace than the German Gestech. The horses ran at the tilt without armour (except for a shaffron), and the lances remained light enough to be wielded without a queue (an exclusively German feature). With its greater speed however, the 'foreign' Gestech still produced spectacular collisions which could result in men and horses knocked down and lance shards thrown high into the air.

▲ The foreign joust of peace (*Welsches Gestech*), preliminary sketch for *Freydal*, *c.*1512–15.
© National Gallery of Art, Washington

RENNEN

Rennen were just as dissimilar as Stechen were to actual battlefield encounters, but as mock jousts of war they were intended to evoke them. Single-pointed lances were used and the tilt was omitted, while the armour, or *Rennzeug*, was made to suggest the silhouette of either partial or complete war harness, depending on the specific type of Rennen course being run. In either case the Rennzeug was thick and heavy, with very little technical similarity to field armour. The horses usually wore no armour apart from a shaffron however, and were free to run much faster than in Stechen. They had to be trained to do so purely on trust however, since they could see nothing – a Rennen shaffron almost always covered the horse's eyes. The distinct contrast

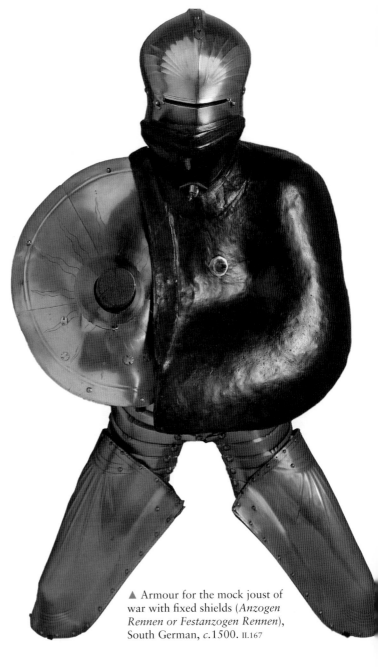

▲ Armour for the mock joust of war with fixed shields (*Anzogen Rennen or Festanzogen Rennen*), South German, *c*.1500. II.167

in speed may explain the characterisation of this class of jousts as Rennen (literally, 'running' or 'race').

Seven recorded forms of the Rennen were run without leg armour. However, when running 'at large', that is without a tilt, the legs were vulnerable, especially the left knee, which could collide with that of the opponent when the horses ran past each other. Furthermore, in such situations it was possible that one or other of the horses would swerve, causing a narrow passing on the wrong side (right to right), in which case the right knees might hit each other. To provide protection against such occurrences, Rennzeuge without full leg

▲ Mock jousts of war with fixed shields, from *Freydal, c.*1512–15. © KHM, Vienna

armour were provided with special plates called *Dilgen*, to protect the upper legs. Shaped to the thighs and knees, Dilgen had been developed from *Streiftartschen* ('swipe-shields') that were flatter, round plates worn on German war armour *c.*1460–90 and also used in the Rennen of that earlier period. Hung on the saddle, Dilgen were designed to remain in place when the rider was unhorsed.

There were many more types of Rennen than there were Stechen courses: fifteen varieties are recorded in pictorial form in *Freydal* and *The Triumph of Maximilian*. These can be distinguished in a number of different ways. First, there are those run in partial armour, which refer to the action of light lancers or *Reiters*, and those in full harness. Most forms involve either a fixed shield, or a 'flying' one, designed to be knocked off if struck well. Some Rennen even incorporated shields and armour built so that they broke apart on impact, throwing specially-made 'shards' of armour into the air with an impressive crash, recalling the exaggerated shattering of armour and splitting of shields routinely described in chivalric romances.

▶ Lance-head for the Rennen, of the 'beaked' type, South German, *c.*1500–10. These distinctive points, or Murneten, were used in most Rennen during the reign of Maximilian. The beak cancels out some of the angle of attack to an opponent passing to the left, allowing the point to strike at closer to ninety degrees to the target. VII.1365

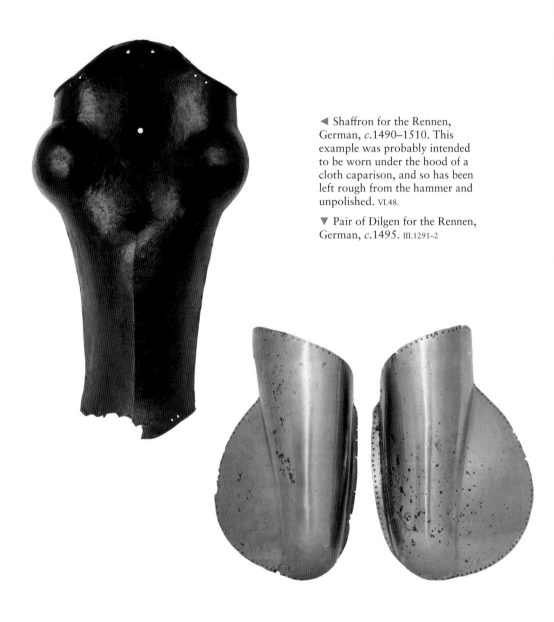

◀ Shaffron for the Rennen, German, *c*.1490–1510. This example was probably intended to be worn under the hood of a cloth caparison, and so has been left rough from the hammer and unpolished. VI.48.

▼ Pair of Dilgen for the Rennen, German, *c*.1495. III.1291–2

Its enthusiastic promotion by the Emperor Maximilian and his successors, his son Philip the Handsome, Archduke of Burgundy and King of Castile (1478–1506), and his grandson the Emperor Charles V (1500–58), enshrined the joust as the supreme form of chivalric combat in the sixteenth century. Their endorsement encouraged other European princes to make it a central part of their own courtly activities, following the Habsburg fashion but also developing it in new directions.

▲ Mock joust of war with flying and exploding shields and leg armour (*Geschifttartschen Rennen*), from *Freydal*, *c*.1512–15. © KHM, Vienna

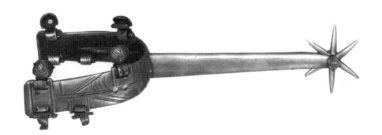

▲ Spur, possibly of the Emperor Maximilian, German, *c*.1500. VI.382

PIECES OF ADVANTAGE

In the fifteenth century and earlier, war armour had tended to develop more rapidly than jousting armour, probably as a result of stronger evolutionary pressures and wider use by many more people. Between 1380 and 1430 for example, the bascinet (the typical helmet worn in battle throughout Europe) had evolved into the great bascinet and sallet, while the helm for the joust of peace had remained largely unchanged for that whole period. Furthermore, the battlefield was a an ever-changing and unpredictable environment, demanding constant improvement in protection. The context of the joust in contrast, essentially, remained the same: they were regulated encounters on horseback, held in controlled conditions, fought one-on-one with the lance.

This closer design relationship between armour for war and for jousting cultivated at the court of Maximilian changed everything. In striving to simulate the appearance of courses run in the equipment of war, while at the same time maintaining a higher level of safety, the Emperor's mock jousts of war increased the rate of development of jousting equipment until it was equivalent to that of war gear. If the courtly Rennen was to continue to fulfil its purpose, of evoking a life-or-death moment in battle, its equipment had to maintain a visual similarity to the latest field armour.

▲ 'Feld Rennen' (field joust), from *The Triumph of Maximilian*, 1516–8. This is an older form of the Feld Rennen, which still employs the sallet, a large wooden Renntartsche and partial steel horse armour.

▲ 'Turnier' (tourney), from *The Triumph of Maximilian*, 1516–8. This is the same equipment used in the later style of Feld Rennen, as illustrated in *Freydal*.

▲ 'Field' joust (Feld Rennen), from *Freydal*, Vienna, *c*.1512–15. © KHM, Vienna

The fulfilment of this new demand can be seen in the 'field' joust (*Feld Rennen*) as conceived under Maximilian. This course looked much like a true battlefield duel in many ways – it was run in the open field, usually on fully-armoured horses, with the riders encased in complete head-to-foot armour surmounted by what was now the most fashionable helmet for the field in Germany – the armet, rather than the sallet which had characterised all older forms of the Rennen. However, the Feld Rennen still cannot be considered a true joust of war, since it involved additional pieces not worn in battle. First and foremost, the left side of the body between the middle of the face and the rein-hand was reinforced with a large steel shield, moulded to the body and affixed to the armour underneath. This piece was a development of older shields for the Rennen (*Renntartschen*), made of wood and faced with iron, leather and textile. These were similarly sculpted to the form of the chin, neck, chest and left arm, one of the best surviving examples being that preserved on the complete Rennzeug in the Royal Armouries collection (see p. 10). Such robust wooden Rennen shields were also employed in earlier forms of the Feld Rennen. Made exclusively in

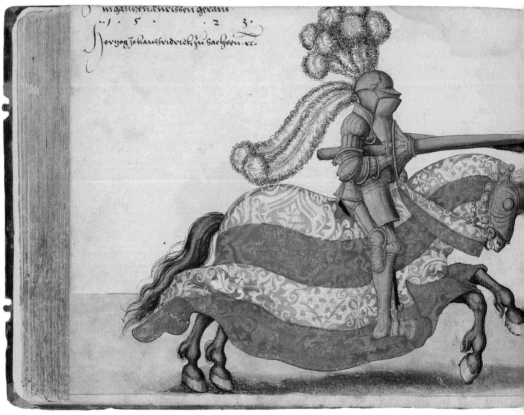

steel, the new 'grandguard' was much lighter than its precursor, and its polished metal surface blended into the rest of the armoured body, making it harder to distinguish from a distance. By *c*.1510, the idea of special moulded reinforces was being extended to the left elbow and forearm. As well as field jousts between individuals, they were also worn in the *Freiturnier* (free tourney), fought in teams and comprising a mass lance charge followed by mêlée combat with swords. Body-formed steel over-plates like this were so effective – being lightweight but strong, and very elegant – that they soon leapt across into jousts of peace, becoming a standard part of armour for those courses from *c*.1530.

◀ Reinforcing pieces for the field joust and free tourney, made by Kolman Helmschmid, Augsburg, *c*.1510–15. © Metropolitan Museum of Art, New York

▼ A 'field' joust (Feld Rennen), in this case run without full horse armour, from the tournament book of Johann Friedrich I of Saxony, made in the workshop of Lucas Cranach the Elder, Wittenberg, *c*.1534–5. © Kunstsammlungen der Veste Coburg, Kupferstickkabinett

THE FOREIGN JOUST OF WAR

A variation of the Feld Rennen, the 'foreign joust of war' (*Welsches Rennen*) was similar in spirit to the Feld Rennen, in that it employed special jousting equipment disguised so as to preserve the outline and appearance of sleek, close-fitting field armour. However, it approached this challenge in a different way. Whereas the armour for the Feld Rennen (and Freiturnier) was essentially actual field armour reinforced with additional plates, that for the foreign Rennen involved a unique style of helmet, the only surviving example of which is preserved in the Royal Armouries.

Designed and built by Lorenz Helmschmid, this remarkable head defence mimics the silhouette of an armet for war, but in fact is constructed like a great bascinet, with the neck transitioning down into a wide base designed to rest on the breast – and backplates to which it was bolted. This system significantly improved protection against whiplash and rotational injury to the head and neck. Simultaneously, when fully assembled with pauldrons and a wooden shield (similar to a *Stechtartsche*) it was

▲ 'Foreign Joust of War' (Welsches Rennen), from *The Triumph of Maximilian*, 1516–8.

impossible to tell the difference between this equipment and a standard field armour. Here, there was no large plate enveloping the whole of the left side of the body; the additional safety precautions were visually even subtler than in the Feld Rennen. This concept represented a perfect balance of security and elegance, and would go on to define certain later classes of armour for the 'foreign' Gestech for almost a hundred years. Like the grandguard, which had evolved from the *Renntartschen* used in mock jousts of war, this style of close-helmet, designed by Maximilian's armourers in Augsburg for an exclusive form of courtly Rennen, would find its ultimate, long-term role in jousts of peace throughout the Renaissance.

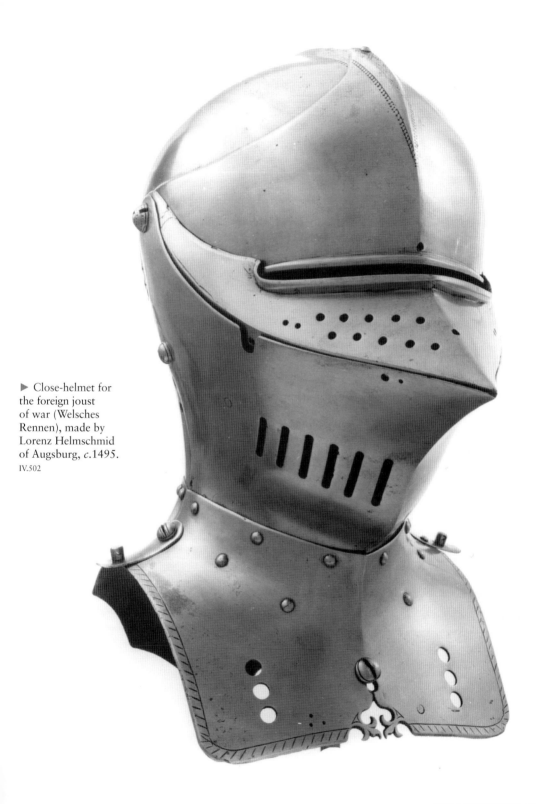

▶ Close-helmet for
the foreign joust
of war (Welsches
Rennen), made by
Lorenz Helmschmid
of Augsburg, *c*.1495.
IV.502

JOUSTING AT THE EARLY TUDOR COURT, *c*.1485–1520

In 1485, Henry of Richmond seized the English crown from King Richard III of the House of York. In so doing he swept away the ancient royal line of Plantagenets and established a new dynasty – the Tudors. For some time, the new regime was itself in danger of being overthrown. Old Yorkist loyalties lingered, and there were many who harboured doubts about the legitimacy of the new ruler's claim to the throne.

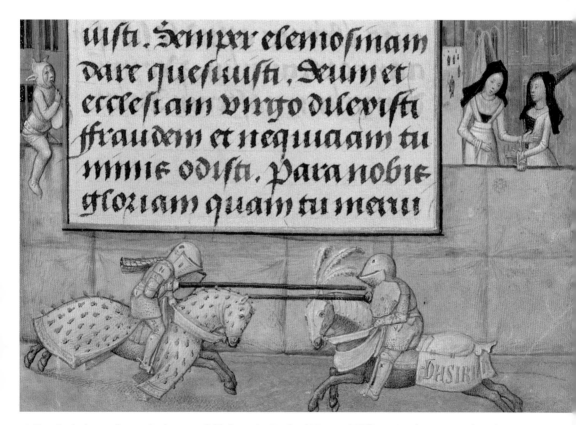

▲ Detail of a joust of peace in the open field, from the Book of Hours of William, Lord Hastings, Flemish, *c*.1480–3. © British Library

Henry VII secured his kingship with military and clandestine operations, economic and political acumen, and propaganda. Jousts were a key part of this last element of his strategy. An extravagant chivalric display was an international statement, of wealth, prestige, and strength. Henry used such events to demonstrate that he was the rightful head of a once turbulent but now stable country. It was he, and not any of his various challengers, who demanded the respect and support of foreign rulers. Jousting spectacles were held at key moments throughout his reign, including his coronation (1485), that of his Queen, Elizabeth of York (1487) and on the occasion of the creation of his eldest son Arthur as Prince of Wales (1489).

▲ Lance-rest or arret, from a West European or Italian armour for the joust of peace, c.1490–1510. III.1706

One of the greatest jousts of the time of Henry VII, held in November 1494, was a response to the notorious plot which had formed around the pretender Perkin Warbeck, who claimed to be Richard Duke of York, younger of the two sons of the Yorkist King Edward IV (d.1483). The Duke had been sent to the Tower of London by Richard III, along with his brother Edward, Prince of Wales (named but never crowned as King Edward V) and both were probably murdered there in the summer of 1483. The counterfeit Duke of York now claimed to be the rightful King of England, and was gathering support on the continent. Henry VII answered this threat by investing his three year-old son (the future King Henry VIII) as Duke of York.

▲ A joust of peace celebrating the meeting of King Christian I of Denmark and Bartolomeo Colleoni at Malpaga in 1474, as imagined by Girolamo Romanino, c.1520.

To celebrate the investiture of the 'real' Duke of York, his father held an extravagant joust at Westminster. This was a grand exhibition of royal confidence, in which a team of English champions committed to 'answer all comers of what nation so ever they be'.

Henry VII held another joust in 1501, to mark the arrival of Katherine of Aragon, bride of his eldest son Arthur, Prince of Wales. Katherine was

▶ Great bascinet for the joust of peace, English or Flemish, *c*.1500. AL.30.3

sister-in-law to the Habsburg Archduke Philip the Handsome, himself an enthusiastic jouster. The challenge for this contest was proclaimed in Burgundy, in Philip's presence, before being sent to France, Spain, Scotland and Germany.

Despite their importance to his royal authority, Henry VII never participated in any of his jousts as a combatant. He may not have had much talent as a martial artist, and therefore wished to avoid the risk of embarrassing upsets in the lists. He also probably felt that his physical safety was too important to hazard in combat. It could also be significant that most of the best jousters at the Henrician court were Yorkists; the uneasy founder of the Tudor dynasty may never have trusted his knights enough to joust with them.

His second son and successor felt differently. The future Henry VIII showed himself to have the makings of a great knight from the age of three, when, to the astonishment of the crowds lining his path, he rode a stallion through London to his investiture as Duke of York. However, the Prince was too important to be allowed to joust. After the premature death of his elder brother, Henry became heir to the throne, and physical risks were out of the question. Nevertheless, he did everything he could to hone his fighting ability. By the age of twelve, and probably earlier, he had a personal master-of-arms, who trained with him every day. On horseback Henry often 'ran at the ring', a newly-invented exercise in which the charging horseman, armed with a short lance but usually without armour, attempted to pick up a small ring of wood, rope or metal suspended over his path. This exercise trained Henry to handle his horse and his weapon simultaneously, whilst also maintaining an awareness of the target, in order to place the lance on it with consistent accuracy. Full armour was occasionally worn to increase the level of difficulty. Even so, for a bellicose young man ring-jousting was no substitute for the real thing.

In 1506 a storm forced Philip, Archduke of Burgundy to land in England. He had been on his way by ship to Spain, to ascend the throne of Castile, when he was waylaid by bad weather. Meeting Philip was a revelation for the boy who would become King Henry VIII. The Archduke was young and charismatic, renowned as a great knight. His departure had been celebrated in Brussels with a magnificent joust at night conducted by torchlight, in which he had jousted against a number of opponents including his father, the Emperor Maximilian. Both broke many spears and showed themselves 'superior to all their opponents'. When he landed in England, all of his armour and jousting equipment came with him. It was all made according to the latest fashions, by German and Flemish masters, and it is possible that Prince Henry was allowed to look at it. Certainly the whole experience of Philip's visit made a profound impression on him.

A NEW KING ENTERS THE LISTS

Henry VII died in 1509, and his only surviving son was crowned King Henry VIII. The new king did not ride in the coronation joust because initially, his ministers insisted that his father's policy of non-participation remain in force. Interestingly however, the first joust of his reign was themed to explore issues relating to the new king's character and the choices he would have to make. A royal team of tenans appeared in the guise of 'scholars', led by a lady dressed as Pallas Athena, the Greco-Roman goddess of wisdom. On the first

▲ Design for a horse armour and costume pieces for a tournament, Anglo-Flemish, *c.*1520. © British Library

day the scholars faced two teams of venans – the 'lovers', led by Cupid, and the 'huntsmen', led by Diana. This joust thus became an embodiment of the forces vying for the king's attention. Would he devote himself to his education, or indulge in sex and blood sports? As it turned out, Henry chose all three.

Obviously the king's councillors were reluctant to condone any royal appearance in the lists. The Tudor chronicler Edward Hall recorded how they felt it was important to 'consider the tender youth of the king, and diverse chances [i.e., risks] of horse and armour', observing that

steel was not so strong, but it might be broken, nor no horse could be so sure of foot, but he may fall.

A KNIGHT DISGUISED

In January 1510, Henry suddenly rejected these concerns and ran his first joust. The event was held at Richmond Palace, and no one was expecting the king to participate. No one, that is, except for Henry himself, his close friend and companion William Compton, and presumably a small team of attendants. In an exploit torn straight out of a medieval romance, Henry and William armed themselves in secret and rode out as 'unknown' knights, carrying no identifying devices or insignia. Their entrance into the field undoubtedly provoked surprise, but the jousts that followed went very well and many spears were broken. However, a swift end was brought to this otherwise successful spectacle when William Compton went up against Sir Edward Neville, one of the best jousters of the time, who was over six feet tall and incredibly strong. Compton was badly injured in their encounter, and during the ensuing commotion a cry went up that it was the king who had been hurt. The unscathed Henry immediately revealed himself, to the amazement of the court. Compton, luckily, made a full recovery.

Henry understood the massive potential impact of a display of his personal fighting prowess. It was the huge political value of his active participation (as well as his indomitable will) that ultimately made it impossible for anyone to stop him from jousting. In March 1510 Henry hosted the first of many displays held in honour of foreign ambassadors. The guests of honour were the envoys of King Ferdinand of Aragon, whose daughter Katherine had been married to Henry's older brother Arthur and who, after her first husband's death, had in turn become Henry's queen in June of the previous year. Henry captained one of the teams, his rich apparel decorated with the devices of Castile and Aragon. In what may have been a concession to his fretting councillors, Henry limited the event to running at the ring, although it seems that, unusually, the participating riders all wore full armour.

By the end of Henry's first regnal year, he was appearing regularly in martial displays of all kinds.

▲ The conclusion of a tournament, French, c.1510. © Sotheby's

Important guests at his court were suitably impressed. In May 1510 Luis Caroz, Spanish ambassador to the English court, reported that

The king of England amuses himself almost every day of the week with running the ring, and with jousts and tournaments on foot ...

There are many young men who excel in this kind of warfare, but the most conspicuous among them all, the most assiduous, and the most interested in the combats is the king himself, who never omits being present at them.

▶ Great bascinet for the joust, Italian, *c.*1500. AL.31

THE WESTMINSTER JOUST OF 1511

▲ The tenans, from the Great Tournament Roll of Westminster, English, *c*.1511. © College of Arms

On 31 December 1510 Katherine of Aragon bore Henry a son, who was christened Henry after his father. As one of many celebrations, the following February the king held a joust at Westminster in Katherine's honour. Portraying himself as a heroic knight in the ancient tradition, Henry expressed his love for the queen through elaborate allegorical combats. The defending tenans at Westminster were four of the best jousters in the realm: Henry himself, Henry's close aide Sir Thomas Knyvet, Lord William Devon (the King's uncle), and the hulking Sir Edward Neville. Each took on the allegorical persona of a different aspect of love. Henry rode as 'Coeur Loyale' ('Loyal Heart'), while the others appeared respectively as 'Valiant Desire', 'Bon Espoir' ('Good Hope'; some accounts call him 'Bon Vouloir' or 'Good Will') and Joyeulx Penser ('Joyful Thought'). The rich pavilions, caparisons and bases of the four challengers were bedecked with golden letter Ks, Queen Katherine's personal monogram, marking them as her devoted servants. Arrayed against them were twenty-one venans, eight on the first day and thirteen on the second. With all of the knights, squires, footmen, musicians and horse attendants clad in cloth of gold, velvet, and silk damask, the Westminster joust represented a magnificence unprecedented in England. Henry spent nearly £4,400 on this event, more than the cost of his favourite warship the *Mary Rose* and similar to £30 million in modern terms.

Strict armour regulations were drawn up for this event. The rules described the requirement as

harness for the tilt without tache or breket, volant pece on the head, Rondell in the gard, Rest of advantage, fraud or deceit or any other mal engine.

Tache is probably another variation on the term *targe* or *tarsche*, referring to the jousting shield. *Breket* is a fifteenth-century term that appears in numerous other English works relating to jousts and tournament combat, and always seems to refer to the arm defences. In this case it probably refers to the *poldermitton* or *manifer*, or both, the specialized arm defences worn – on the right and left arms respectively – in jousts of peace from the late 1400s onwards. The *Volant pece on the hed* was a reinforcing brow plate.

▲ Great bascinet for the joust, West European (probably Flemish), *c*.1510–20. IV.593

Rondell in the gard refers simply to the *vamplate*, the circular metal hand-guard often fitted to the lance from the mid fourteenth century, while *Rest of advantaige* is the lance-rest or arret.

The banning of all of these items, but especially the last, was somewhat unusual. However, these stipulations are largely borne out by the illustrations in the *Westminster Roll*, the official visual record of the event, now in the College of Arms in London.

Although lance-rests are shown in some instances, shields are entirely absent, as are special defences for the arms – all of the jousters appear to be wearing standard field vambraces and gauntlets. The helms have brow-reinforces, while the lances are not fitted with vamplates. The disallowing of standard safety measures built into the armour for the joust of peace may have been a characteristically English rejection of continental trends or precautions, a demonstration of the toughness of Henry and his knights. On the other hand, the prohibition of lance-rests somewhat negates the apparently increased level of danger, since without them the jousters would not have been able to strike each other very hard. The lances themselves may also have been quite light, so that the jousters had a chance of breaking them without arrets. The score sheets or *cheques* from Westminster survive,

▲ Henry VIII jousting before Katherine of Aragon, from the Great Tournament Roll of Westminster, English, *c*.1511. © College of Arms

and record a high number of attaints (good blows to the opponent which do not break the lance) over the two days of jousting, while a much lower number of lances were broken. These results were almost certainly due to the prohibition of the energy-conducting arret; in many cases well-placed lances were undoubtedly knocked out of the jousters' hands before they could be compelled to break.

Under the Queen's gaze, King Henry delivered powerful blows to his opponents and received theirs in turn, safely and skilfully, as described in *The Great Chronicle of London*:

Anon the king called for a spear and so ran six courses or he left. And broke in those six courses four spears as well and as valiantly as any man of arms might break them. And such as were broken upon him, he received them as though he had felt no dint of any stroke.

The author of this account is slightly mistaken, in his scoring if not in spirit. The cheques indicate that Henry never broke more than three lances in any of his sets, although he routinely struck four or five times in sets of six courses. The king was certainly hitting more accurately and more consistently than most of his knights. In his total of twenty-four courses on the first day, Henry scored two attaints to the head, seven attaints to the body, and seven lances broken on the body. He therefore missed eight times, or, in a third of his courses. His miss-rate may seem high, but it must be evaluated in context. Several of the king's misses may have occurred in attempts to strike his opponent's head, by far the more difficult of the two primary targets available to him (the other being the left shoulder and upper body). Despite his numerous unsuccessful courses, Henry's record was still superior to that of any of the other tenans: Lord William Devon ran nine courses but only scored five hits yielding one lance broken on the head (the only one of the day), one attaint to the head and three attaints to the body. Sir Thomas Knyvet ran eleven courses and struck his opponents five times, achieving two lances broken on the body and three attaints to the body, while Sir Edward Neville ran just one set of six courses and only managed a single hit (a lance broken on the body). On average their opponents scored with similar frequencies, managing between one and three hits in each set of six courses. The most unfortunate or inexperienced venan, Christopher Willoughby, appears to have missed every time despite being granted two additional courses in his set.

On the second day Henry jousted even more enthusiastically, running 28 courses (four sets of six courses and two sets of two, these last short sets being run specially for 'the Kinge's ladies sake') and scoring 22 hits comprising one attaint to the head, nine attaints to the body and twelve lances broken on the body. The averages of the others remained more or less the same, although three jousters each managed to break a lance on their opponents' heads, a feat worth 'ii speres well broken' or double the points of a lance broken on the body. The large number of misses could indicate a lack of skill, although it may instead, in some cases, reflect the keenness of the participants to strike the head, with the vast majority of attempts failing. If the latter explanation is correct, Henry could be seen as something of a 'safe player', preferring to score a higher number of easier hits to a fewer number of difficult ones. For the vast majority of spectators, the technicalities meant nothing: all that mattered was that they saw their king shattering more lances than anyone else.

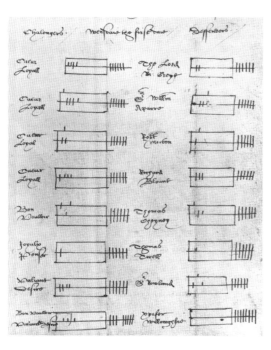

▲ Score cheque from the first day of the Westminster Joust, English, 12 February 1511. © College of Arms

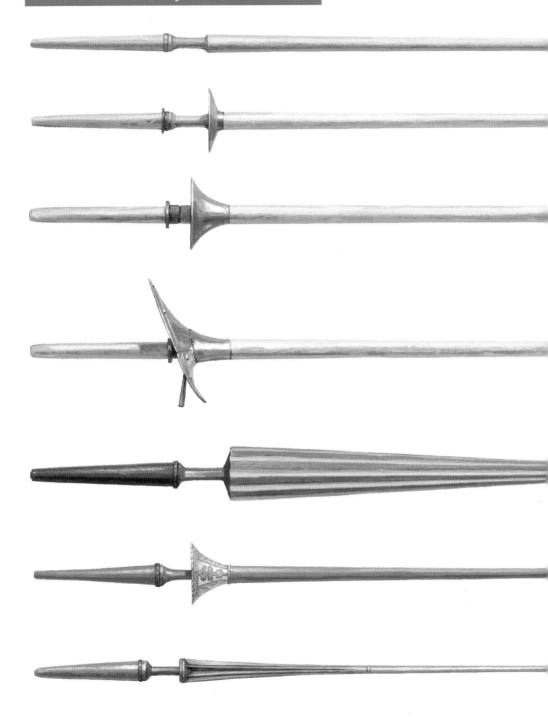

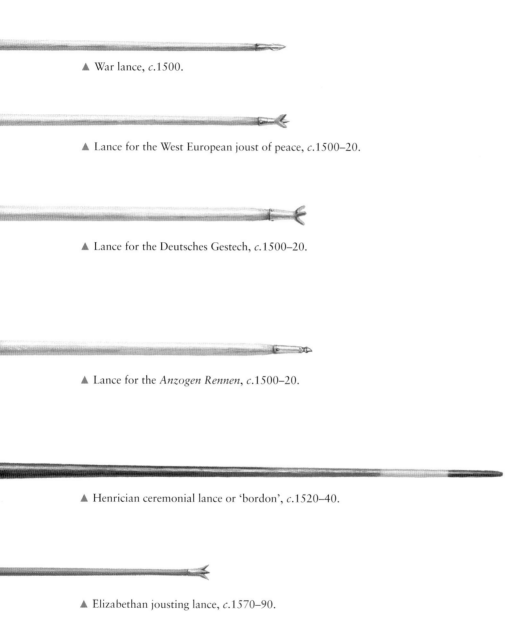

▲ War lance, *c*.1500.

▲ Lance for the West European joust of peace, *c*.1500–20.

▲ Lance for the Deutsches Gestech, *c*.1500–20.

▲ Lance for the *Anzogen Rennen*, *c*.1500–20.

▲ Henrician ceremonial lance or 'bordon', *c*.1520–40.

▲ Elizabethan jousting lance, *c*.1570–90.

▲ French jousting lance, *c*.1610–30.

The Royal Armouries collection includes three extremely rare lances dating from the reign of Henry VIII. Richly decorated in gold, they are of a remarkable size, the largest being nine inches in diameter above the grip and over fourteen feet long. Notably, they are hollow. This observation has encouraged the common misconception that jousting lances were often made this way, to lighten them and allow them to break safely and easily. However, these lances are needlessly large, at least from a practical jousting point of view. Their hollowness does reduce their weight to some extent, but they are still very heavy, around 20 lbs each. It is just possible to carry them, but their great weight and size makes them excessively unwieldy and therefore unsafe for practical use.

In reality, descriptions in Tudor documents describe these massive lances as being carried onto the field as part of the opening procession and pageantry that preceded Henrician jousts, but they are not used to strike opponents in the courses themselves. The revels accounts of Henry's reign refer to them as *great spears* or *boordons*. In a joust at Greenwich on 7 July 1517, held to entertain visiting Flemish diplomats, Sir Nicholas Carew, Master of the Horse, appeared in the guise of 'The Blue Knight' and, as the accounts state, 'ran with the great boordon'. This seems to have been a solo parade act, a demonstration of prowess. Carew may even have run at the ring with his massive lance, but jousting was out of the question; no one else was involved in the demonstration.

Philippe de Commines, an important eyewitness at many key moments in Franco–Burgundian history during the late fifteenth century, states that at the Battle of Fornovo in 1495, many of the Italian men-at-arms opposing the invading French forces were armed with colourful lances,

▲ Great lance or 'boordon', traditionally associated with Charles Brandon, Duke of Suffolk, English, c.1520–40. VII.550

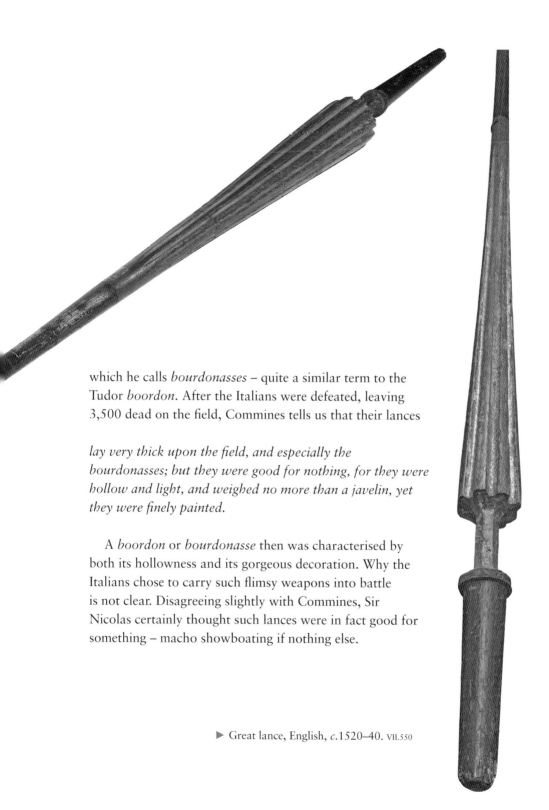

which he calls *bourdonasses* – quite a similar term to the Tudor *boordon*. After the Italians were defeated, leaving 3,500 dead on the field, Commines tells us that their lances

lay very thick upon the field, and especially the bourdonasses; but they were good for nothing, for they were hollow and light, and weighed no more than a javelin, yet they were finely painted.

A *boordon* or *bourdonasse* then was characterised by both its hollowness and its gorgeous decoration. Why the Italians chose to carry such flimsy weapons into battle is not clear. Disagreeing slightly with Commines, Sir Nicolas certainly thought such lances were in fact good for something – macho showboating if nothing else.

▶ Great lance, English, *c.*1520–40. VII.550

▲ The lists at the Field of Cloth of Gold, *c.*1545. © Royal Collection Trust / Her Majesty Queen

In June 1520, King Henry VIII of England and King Francis I of France met in the Pas de Calais in one of the grandest diplomatic occasions of the age. Masterminded by England's chief minister and papal legate Cardinal Thomas Wolsey, the meeting was intended to create a lasting peace between the two kingdoms, after hundreds of years of conflict. The area known historically as The Vale of Gold had been used for attempts at Anglo-French reconciliation since the Middle Ages. Wolsey's 'Field of Cloth of Gold' was now, optimistically, conceived as a key element of the dream of outlawing all war between Christians. However, beneath the veneer of a peace summit, each royal party sought to outdo and even intimidate the other, with the size of their retinues, the richness of their clothes, tents and accoutrements, the quality and ingeniousness of their hospitality and the fighting skill of their lords and knights. Above everything else, the Field of Cloth of Gold was a courtly combat spectacle, with scores of English and French noblemen competing in armoured combat on foot, mounted tourneys and jousts.

Given the nature of the event, it have might been expected that any encounters in the lists would be run as jousts of peace. However, that is not exactly what took place. The French stipulated that the jousting should follow what was then the prevailing fashion at the court of Francis I. The courses were to be run at the tilt and, as the printed terms of the joust stated:

In consequence of the numerous accidents to noblemen, sharp steel [is] not to be used as in times past, but only arms for strength, agility and pastime.

The field then was set for jousts of peace, with a tilt and lances of courtesy, tipped with coronels. However, the participants were to be equipped in the armour of war, including full horse armour (accounts of the event refer specifically to the jousters riding 'barded' or armoured horses). The risks of a true joust of war in the open field with war lances would be reduced, while at the same time, the accomplishment of the participants in the use of battle gear would be thoroughly demonstrated. In this way the jousts held at the Field of the Cloth of Gold fitted the spirit of the occasion – openly cordial and obliquely belligerent.

The French ordinance for the 1520 joust also clarified that while no shields were to be used, the field armours could include reinforcing plates:

▲ Jacques de Lalaing jousting with a Sicilian Knight before the Duke of Burgundy, from a manuscript version of the *Livre des faits de Jacques de Lalaing, c.1530.*
© The J. Paul Getty Museum, Los Angeles

By field armours with pieces of advantage [we] mean that everyone should wear an armet and no other head gear. That is to say no helm, no half-helm and no bascinet. Concerning the rest of the pieces of advantage it is whatever venans and tenans wish to wear.

Although the use of war armour at the tilt might seem strange, it was actually one of the most typical joust forms throughout western Europe in the early sixteenth century, having endured since the introduction of the tilt a hundred years before. Beyond the general machismo of such courses, jousts in war armour had the additional advantage that they facilitated much larger numbers of participants. Many more knights could take part, beyond the richest lords, since everyone already had field armour for other reasons. Specialised armour for the joust of peace however, was expensive and used only on rare occasions, and had no other potential use. For many, the cost of such equipment was too great, or it simply could not be justified. If the aim of the French regulations was to encourage large numbers of knights to participate, it certainly worked. The kings of England and France together led a team of sixteen tenans (seven English and seven French knights, in addition to the two kings). Arrayed against them were 145 venans, organised into fourteen teams each numbering between ten and twelve knights. The organisers planned well for this abundant display of jousting talent, ordering 1,000 vamplates and 2,000 coronels (also called *mornes*).

Interestingly, although the English in general abided by the French rules, they did make certain changes. The anonymous eyewitness account 'La Description et ordre du camp, festins et jousts', written while the event was still in progress, notes that:

[I] cannot write of the jousts as they are not yet over. The lists were made with counter lists in the French fashion but at the request of the king of England, the counter-lists were taken away.

Beyond the requirement that each jouster be armed in field harness, it is interesting that the French left the precise arrangement of reinforcing plates to the individual's discretion. War armour of this period was already optimised for heavy cavalry combat, with the visored armet worn with a reinforcing bevor or 'wrapper' which gave additional protection to the lower face and throat, and a large, shield-like gardbrace fitted to the left shoulder, a continuation of the asymmetrical concept for knightly armour developed *c.*1410–35. Between *c.*1490 and 1510, the left gardbrace had grown very large indeed, with a high vertical neck-guard or *haute-piece*. This was an advantageous piece to have in heavy cavalry encounters on the battlefield, for which it was primarily

▲ Effigy of Sir Roger Tocotes (d.1492), Church of St. Nicholas, Bromham, Wiltshire.

▲ Armour for war, joust and tournament, Italian, *c.*1520. © Musée de l'Armée, Paris

intended, although such a plate was also just as appropriate in the joust. This especially large left gardbrace may have been called the *grandguard* as early as 1520. Indeed, in the official account of the Field of Cloth of Gold, Edward Hall describes how the English king broke the shoulder reinforce of his opponent:

The king of England was ready and struck his horse with the spurs and so fiercely ran to the counter party [the Duke of Bourbon] that his grand guard was lost with the great stroke that the king gave him.

Otherwise Hall almost never refers to any specifics regarding the armour worn in the jousts, except in order to record the damage inflicted by Henry on his opponents' equipment. In another important passage, it is a 'charnel' (in this context, one of the visor pivots) that is broken:

Then ran the king of England to Monsire Graundeuile with great vigour, so that the spear broke in the king's hand to the vamplate all to shivers. And at the second course he gave the said Monsire Graundeuile such a stroke that the charnel of his head piece, although the same was very strong, was broken in suchwise that he might run no more.

The misfortune of Monsire Graundeuile aside, within the stipulation that each jouster must wear an armet, and no other type of helmet, there was room to enhance the capacity of one's head-piece to resist lance attack. This is demonstrated by three contemporary helmets in the Royal Armouries Collection. The first two are typical Anglo–Flemish armets of the period, which close around the wearer's face by means of cheek-pieces hinged to the sides of a ridged and frontally-reinforced skull. Interestingly, both of these helmets have visors made in much the same way as the face-plates of a jousting helm, with an integral brow reinforce or *volant piece*, which, together with the skull and separate brow plate underneath, forms a triple-layer of steel over the forehead. Also, perhaps most characteristically, the lower edge of the sight forms a lip projecting beyond the upper edge designed to protect the wearer's eyes from lance-points and fragments moving upwards after an impact on the chest, shoulder or lower face. Such a visor might not have been designed exclusively for jousting, and would certainly have been most efficacious in heavy cavalry warfare. Indeed, such things do appear in contemporary Flemish depictions of warfare. Nevertheless, the design was better suited to jousting than other armet visor types. The exchange of a lighter, more ventilated field visor for one of these heavier, joust-like visors would certainly have been within the rules at the Field of Cloth of Gold.

The third helmet is probably English or Flemish. Unlike the other two it is unambiguously a jousting helmet, although it maintains a profile quite similar to that of a field armet. Technically however it is a close-helmet, according to the modern definition, having a one-piece chin-plate or bevor pivoted on the same points as the visor. The hasps at the sides which secure the bevor to the sides of the skull are very strongly built, while the skull itself, just behind the join on either side, includes pairs of holes intended for pointing tight the brow band and chin-strap of a special form of padded lining designed for jousting. Finally the visor is fitted with an additional reinforce over its integral brow plate, an unusual feature not found on field helmets, and the sight has been made with a pronounced squint on the left side (the area most vulnerable to piercing by lances in the joust). This testifies to an awareness of the threat to the jouster's eyes, especially on the left side. Although it is not technically an armet, this helmet is quite similar in its form and performance, another example of specialised jousting equipment masquerading as field armour. Such a thing may still have been allowable at the Field of Cloth of Gold, unless it was what the French ordinance meant by a half-helm, which was disallowed. Regardless, this curious piece faithfully follows the international fashion of the first half of the sixteenth century for jousts in war gear subtly enhanced for greater safety in ways which did not significantly alter the overall appearance of the armour.

Despite the undoubtedly good intentions of the organisers, the Field of Cloth of Gold was a diplomatic failure. Soon after, the English renewed their alliance

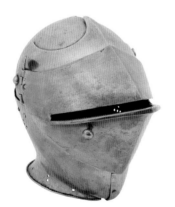

▲ Armet, Flemish, c.1510. IV.576

▲ The Battle of Lokeren, from a manuscript version of *Livre des faits de Jacques de Lalaing*, c.1530. © The J. Paul Getty Museum, Los Angeles

▲ Armet, Flemish, c.1510. IV.1601

with Charles V, who declared war on France the following year. The Italian War of 1521–5 culminated in the catastrophic defeat of the French at the Battle of Pavia, where many of the noblemen who had accompanied Francis I to the Field in 1520 were killed, and the French king himself was taken prisoner and remained in captivity for over a year.

► Close-helmet for the joust, English or Flemish, c.1520. The sight of this helmet has a pronounced 'squint' on the left side, where lance impacts were most likely to land, to better protect the wearer's eyes. IV.413.

HENRY VIII AND THE ROYAL WORKSHOP AT GREENWICH

In the initial years of his reign, Henry VIII impressed the world with his lavish jousts and specifically, with his personal prowess in the lists. Unlike the other great Renaissance princes of his time however, such as the Emperor Maximilian and King Francis I of France, Henry had no court armourers, no royal workshop producing advanced armour for war, tournaments, parades, and jousts. Instead, he was forced to follow the technological and artistic lead of other armourers working for foreign princes, in Austria, Italy and Flanders. This intolerable situation restricted Henry's personal access to the best equipment, while also hampering his ability to participate fully in international courtly relations. Fine armours were often given as diplomatic gifts, as a way for the most powerful rulers to demonstrate the strength of their domestic military infrastructure, while also flaunting their personal wealth, taste, and largesse. England had skilled armourers, especially in London, but Henry's domestic craftsmen worked in the local styles and tradition of his father's and grandfather's time. Their products were of a good quality, but they were artistically and technologically conservative. English armour in the early sixteenth century was therefore ill-suited to the international world of diplomatic gift-giving, and certainly was not innovative enough for the fashion-conscious, continentally-oriented young king. Henry needed something revolutionary, and unique. In his quest to create a court armoury in England, Henry first sent to Milan for armourers in 1511, but he seems to have been dissatisfied with Italian work. Between 1512 and 1515 he recruited armourers from Flanders, the great South German centres of Augsburg, Nuremberg, Landshut, and possibly also from Cologne and Brunswick in northern Germany. The Germans and Flemings pleased him better, and by 1515, Henry had founded his royal court workshop, staffed by his 'Almain' armourers. Initially they were based at Southwark, which had been a centre of armour-making since the previous century. Here a new style of armour began to be devised, undoubtedly with enthusiastic input from

◄ Chess piece, West European, possibly English, c.1510–30. © Metropolitan Museum of Art, New York

Henry himself, collaborating with his court armourers in much the same way as did his role model, the Emperor Maximilian. In fact, the first armour assembled by the Almains was a fusion of Henry's two strongest influences at that moment.

The 'silvered and engraved' armour, one of the great treasures of the Royal Armouries collection, is predominantly Italo–Flemish in style, the prevailing fashion in England during the early sixteenth century. However, it incorporates, uniquely, a steel base of the Innsbruck type, undoubtedly modelled on one that formed part of a gift armour made by Konrad Seusenhofer and presented by Maximilian to Henry in 1514. The result of this design composition is magnificent, if slightly jarring – a collage of two very distinct styles. Later Henrician armours would finesse the fusion of Italianate and German features to create something new: Henry's personal court style. At some point just after March 1520 the Almain armourers were relocated to their permanent home in Greenwich, at the 'Palace of Placentia' on the banks of the Thames, which would endure as a production centre of the finest quality armour for more than a hundred years.

As well as making harness for the king's personal use, the Greenwich armourers also provided their master with the ability to present fine armours as gifts, to foreign noblemen, diplomats and Henry's close friends and supporters. Although it is probable that Henry and perhaps other English noblemen wore armours made by the king's Almains in the jousts held at the Field of Cloth of Gold in 1520, none survive. However, a good sense of the emergent Greenwich style is found on a field armour made in *c.*1525, possibly as a gift for Robert III de la Marck, Maréchal de Fleuranges, now in the Musée de l'Armée, Paris. Henry had fought with Fleuranges at the Field of Cloth of Gold, and broken his pauldron; the gift therefore may have been a generous way of honouring a memorable combat. Other evidence of Henry's gift-giving may be found in a portrait of the English courtier Sir Nicholas Carew, painted by the court artist Hans Holbein the Younger in the early 1530s. Here the pauldrons and vambraces are closely similar both to those of the Fleuranges armour. However this armour is marked out as a heavy cavalry armour or even a light jousting armour by the presence of haute-pieces on both shoulders, an antebrachial guard for the right elbow (to prevent hyperextension) and a quite substantial lance-rest.

◀ The 'silvered and engraved' equestrian armour of Henry VIII, made at Greenwich incorporating Flemish elements, 1514-5. II.5.

All of these features are found on the next surviving Greenwich armour in the chronological sequence after the Fleuranges armour. On 10 March 1524, Henry rode into the lists in 'a new armour made to his own design and fashion, such as no armourer before that time had seen'. This revolutionary creation does not survive, but its description emphasises the experimental nature of activity at Greenwich, while also testifying to the king's personal involvement in the design process. This lost 1524 armour must have looked quite similar to another, slightly later one made for Henry three years later, preserved today in the Metropolitan Museum of Art in New York. He apparently wore this armour in jousts held on Shrove Tuesday (5 March) 1527, where it was mentioned by the chronicler Edward Hall (using similar terms to how the 1524 armour was described) as a 'new harness all gilt of a strange fashion that had not been seen'. This armour is very impressive, most obviously because it is fully etched and gilt over its entire surface. This most extreme extent of decoration was rare even on royal armours. However it was technically very innovative as well, as Hall implies. For this is not just one armour, it is a garniture, including a coherent system of exchange pieces designed to configure the armour for field, joust and tournament use.

◀ Sir Nicholas Carew, by Hans Holbein the Younger, 1532
© Drumlanrig Castle Thornhill, Scotland

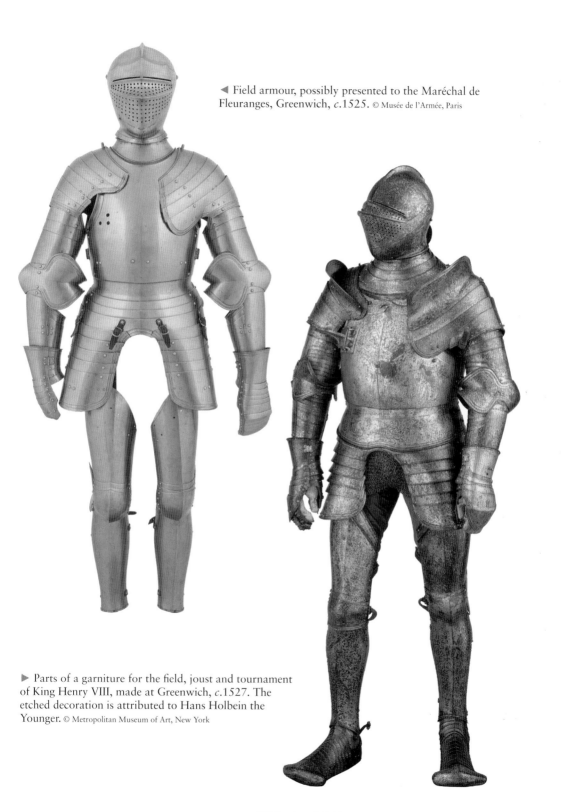

◄ Field armour, possibly presented to the Maréchal de Fleuranges, Greenwich, *c*.1525. © Musée de l'Armée, Paris

▶ Parts of a garniture for the field, joust and tournament of King Henry VIII, made at Greenwich, *c*.1527. The etched decoration is attributed to Hans Holbein the Younger. © Metropolitan Museum of Art, New York

THE RENAISSANCE GARNITURE

By 1520, European noblemen were increasingly required to fight in different ways beyond their traditional roles as heavy cavalry and fully-armoured infantry. Maximilian had already popularised the idea of a commander fighting in the press with his professional infantrymen, while at the same time, the considerable advantages of fast-moving, longer-range light and medium cavalry were quickly being realised. At court, after the example set at the Field of Cloth of Gold, martial spectacles increasingly involved jousting of several forms, tourney combat (both between individuals and teams) and foot combat in many different weapons forms. Each of these disciplines required specific harness. Building on the emergent technology of 'pieces of advantage' (which were initially just reinforces added to the basic field armour) to better serve the combat needs of the Renaissance knight, armourers perfected what is

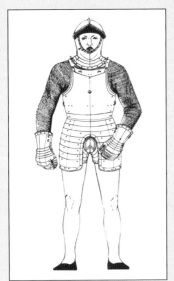

▲ War: Infantry

▲ War: Demi-Lancer

▲ War: Heavy Cavalry

now termed the *garniture* around 1525. This was a system built around an armour (or series of armours decorated *en suite*), comprised of a range of specialised parts or *pieces of exchange*. Some of these pieces were still additional over-plates, while others were alternative elements of differing construction. These could be used to re-configure the harness for any one of a diversity of fighting styles. One armour could now serve many roles. Smaller garnitures provided only the parts required for war. Field armour was also used in certain joust forms, but the most prestigious festivals often involved highly-specialised courses, such as the joust of peace. Therefore, the wealthy now indulged in the luxury of much larger garnitures which could be used for all battlefield roles but which also incorporated exchange pieces for the various jousts, the tourney, and formal combats on foot.

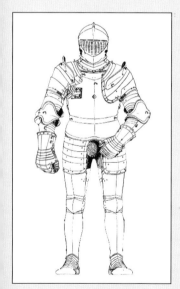  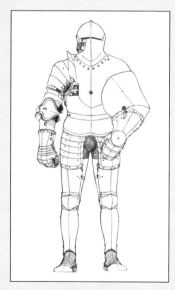

▲ Tourney and Joust of War   ▲ Formal Foot Combat   ▲ Joust of Peace

In his early years, Henry's personal fighting ability helped to construct a public image of him as the heroic champion of his people, while in the eyes of visiting ambassadors he seemed intimidating and invincible. The creation of such a reputation had its risks however. In 1524 Henry narrowly escaped death in a joust with Charles Brandon, Duke of Suffolk. Upon completion of a new jousting armour (the lost 1524 garniture mentioned above), Henry was keen 'to test the [armour] at the tilt, and ordered a joust for the purpose'. This was perhaps the first time he had worn this equipment, made according to a new design, and he was unfamiliar with it. This may have been the first time Henry had worn a helmet with a two-part visor, where the upper half could be raised while the lower half remained in the closed position in front of the face. Henry forgot to lower the upper visor of his helmet, and as the two

▲ A joust at the tilt, from a manuscript recording the regulations for 'the jousts of peace royal', English, c.1550. This drawing in fact illustrates the engagement incorrectly, showing the jousters passing right side to right side, with the lances held in their left hands. It has been mirrored here to show the action as it would have occurred in reality. Note that both jousters are aiming for their opponent's heads. Also, the action is being fought in field armour without shields but with coronels. © College of Arms

jousters encountered each other, Suffolk, who had been having problems seeing out of his own helmet, struck the king in the head just above the eyes. The lance shattered upon striking the edge of the skull of Henry's helmet, and a number of splinters entered the King's face-opening. As the eyewitness account of Edward Hall observes, 'there was great danger of death since the face was bare'. Amazingly, the king came through untouched. Hall continues:

The armourers were much blamed for this, and so was the lord marquise [Suffolk] for delivering the spear blow when his face was open, but the king said that no one was to blame but himself …

Then the king called his armourers and put all his pieces of armour together and then took a spear and ran six courses very well, by which all men could see that he had taken no hurt, which was a great joy and comfort to all his subjects present.

Henry was extremely lucky that day, as he undoubtedly realised in private after the action was over. He was not so fortunate twelve years later. In 1536, he was severely injured while running at the ring in the Greenwich tiltyard. There are three surviving accounts of what happened next. The herald Charles Wriothesley records that 'the King ran that time at the ring and had a fall from his horse'. The Imperial ambassador Eustace Chapuys, related that 'the King being mounted on a great horse to run at the lists, both fell so heavily that everyone thought it a miracle he was not killed'. Interestingly, even distant gossip at the French court, several times removed from any eyewitness (as noted by Pedro Ortiz, the Emperor Charles V's ambassador in Rome) had it simply that 'The French king said that the king of England had fallen from his horse, and been for two hours without speaking'. Regardless of the account, Henry was evidently knocked senseless and remained unconscious for several hours. It has been suggested that the King's brain was damaged in the accident, since those who were close to him observed that his character was much altered afterwards. He suffered terrible headaches and violent mood swings, and, no doubt depressed by his impaired physical state, his weight increased and his health declined.

Because it happened in a tiltyard, many have since assumed (wrongly) that this misfortune took place during a joust. However, Wriothesley explicitly states that Henry was running at the ring, one of several exercises run 'in the lists' as Chapuys mentioned. No opponent or lance encounter was mentioned by anyone, and no joust at Greenwich is recorded as having occurred anywhere near the time of the accident on 24 January. Furthermore, had Henry been armed in one of his fine Greenwich armours, he would have been well-protected and almost certainly would have emerged unscathed. However, ring courses were generally run without armour.

THE 1540 GARNITURE OF HENRY VIII

Of all the armours made for Henry VIII at Greenwich, the '1540' garniture – the date is etched on the front of the gorget – is the most complete today. It was made by (and under the supervision of) Erasmus Kyrkener, a Flemish armourer who had been with the workshop almost from the beginning. He had attended the king at the Field of Cloth of Gold, and was appointed Master Workman (head armourer) probably during the 1530s. The 1540 garniture is a superb example of the armourer's art; despite the fact that Henry was seriously overweight by the late 1530s, the armour succeeds in disguising the true extent of his corpulent form, at least from the front, by means of careful manipulation of the body's proportions and silhouette. Nevertheless, it is a massive armour.

The 1540 garniture was large in extent as well as in stature, although a number of its exchange pieces are now missing. Enough of the armour survives however to give a good impression of how it could be used. As well as at least two battlefield configurations, for infantry and cavalry combat, the 1540 garniture also provided for a full range of joust and tournament applications: foot combat (both in the champ clos and at the barriers), tourney, and the joust of peace, or 'joust royal'. Of all the possible configurations, that for the joust was the heaviest. Over a thick cavalry breastplate (which does not survive) went the heavy grandguard, a sculpted shield of steel skilfully moulded to the form of the chest, left shoulder,

▲ Henry VIII's 1540 garniture configured for the joust, showing the complex ventilation method on the right side of the face.

and lower face. The right side of the grandguard has been fashioned into a vertical flange designed to protect the vulnerable right shoulder from lances skating across the body. The helmet was fitted with a special jousting visor, made much thicker than the field visor. A unique feature of the jousting visor of the 1540 armour is the bulbous right side, which is cut with several rows of closely-spaced diagonal slots, to ensure good ventilation. This ventilation area fits snugly into the grandguard, which provides another short flange to protect the slotted area from lance-points and flying splinters. Below the visor, the grandguard is also fitted with a trio of aerating cut-outs, each guarded by a door-like plate resembling the aileron of an aircraft. The sights of the jousting visor are also very narrow; the design of the whole head area gives the impression that the armourer was instructed to provide total protection against accidental

◀ Garniture for war, joust and tournament of Henry VIII, made at Greenwich under Erasmus Kyrkener, 1540. The decoration is attributed to Hans Holbein the Younger. II.8

injury, especially from splinters, while providing the king with plenty of fresh air.

The jousting configuration of the 1540 garniture also incorporated a dedicated pair of vambraces, built heavier than the field versions, with the right fitted with the antebrachial guard for the elbow which by now was a standard Greenwich feature. The left arm was reinforced with a *pasguard*, onto the lower edge of which is strapped the *manifer*, or jousting gauntlet for the left hand. The centre of the manifer is further strengthened with a small disk-shaped reinforce or *rondel*.

The missing cavalry breastplate would have been fitted with staples near the right arm-pit to support the lance-rest, while key-hole slots in its lower edge would have accepted the turn-pins fitted to the cavalry skirt

▲ The second set of exchange pieces for the joust from the 1540 garniture. Apart from small variations in the etched decoration, they are identical to the other set of joust pieces.

and tassets. The tassets designed for riding are shorter than the pair for foot combat, and were worn in all mounted configurations, including the joust, along with the extended cuisses of exchange.

One curious aspect of the 1540 garniture is that it includes double sets of all the exchange pieces for the joust and tourney: two grandguards, two pasguards (one of which is now lost), two manifers, two jousting visors and two locking gauntlets. Such pairs of identical parts are found on no other surviving garniture, and their presence here is at first hard to explain. Henry's jousting career was for the most part over by 1540, so the second set of jousting pieces cannot have been required as spares in the event that the first pair were heavily damaged. One explanation could be that the 1540 garniture, although it was a fully-functional armour of the highest quality, was first and foremost a symbol of power – apparent proof of the king's enduring physical strength at a time when his health and fitness were rapidly declining. This armour promoted the illusion that Henry was strong and vigorous, and therefore, by implication, still a powerful ruler. The visual reinforcement of this message was urgently needed in 1540.

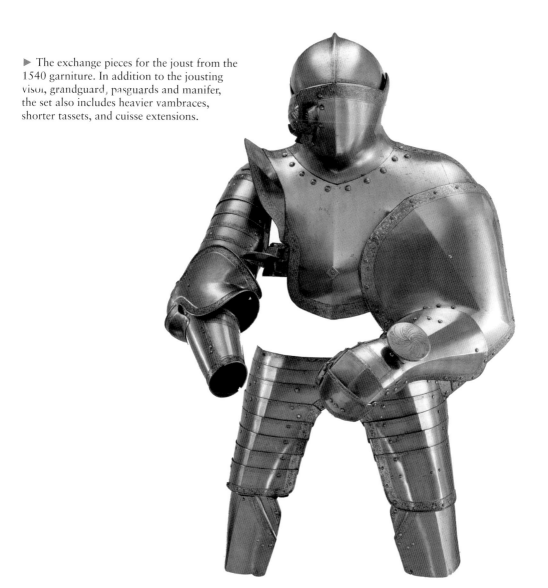

▶ The exchange pieces for the joust from the 1540 garniture. In addition to the jousting visor, grandguard, pasguards and manifer, the set also includes heavier vambraces, shorter tassets, and cuisse extensions.

By this time, although he did enjoy periods of recovery, Henry was in fact becoming increasingly immobilised by obesity, illness and the long-term effects of old injuries. This extraordinary armour, beautifully etched and gilt according to designs by Henry's court artist, Hans Holbein, was essentially an expensive public relations exercise, a glittering denial of the King's looming infirmity. The additional (and redundant) pieces of exchange were probably intended to make the garniture appear – superficially – as rich, extensive and complicated as possible.

Although the technology of the garniture appeared quite early in England during the mid 1520s, it is likely that the concept was first developed in Germany, probably by master armourers in Augsburg. This finely etched and gilt garniture was made there around forty years after the idea for pieces of advantage first appeared *c.*1500, making it a contemporary of Henry VIII's 1540 armour. The core field armour is today preserved in the Royal Armouries, while most of the exchange pieces known to survive are in the Wallace Collection. It was probably made for Hans Walther von Hürnheim (d.1557), a nobleman from Kirchheim in central Germany. The Hürnheim coat of arms, a pair of golden stag's antlers on a red field, is displayed on the shaffron, and Hans Walther was the member of this family most likely

▲ Field components of the Hürnheim garniture,
Augsburg, *c.*1540. II.187

to have commissioned such a rich and extensive garniture. He was a member of the Order of the Knights of the Golden Spur, made up of the elite officers of the German Empire, an important official in the government of the Emperor Charles V, and a powerful military commander with a force of ten thousand *Landsknecht* mercenaries at his disposal. The very striking decorative scheme of his armour features etched and gilt strapwork bands containing lines of chevrons, picked out alternately in gilt and white steel. Finely-etched pomegranates are enclosed within the gilt chevrons.

In addition to the usual infantry and light, medium and heavy cavalry configurations, this chevron garniture was designed to be used in at least three different types of joust and tournament. The surviving jousting pieces are intended for the new forms of 'foreign' joust coming into fashion in the German Empire at this time, which were run in both *Stechen* (tilt) and *Rennen* (no tilt) variants.

▲ Pieces of exchange for the Welsches Rennen and demi-shaffron of the Hürnheim garniture, Augsburg, *c.*1540. © The Wallace Collection, London

One of the three German interpretations of 'foreign' jousting fashions, a new iteration of the *Welsches Rennen*, was actually quite a faithful emulation of the latest Italian style. It involved a reinforcing bevor for the lower face; a *grandguard* closely-moulded to the shoulder and chest; a large *pasguard* to protect the left elbow; and a *gauntlet reinforce*, having a wide, flaring cuff, which was bolted on over the standard field gauntlet to enhance the protection of the left hand and forearm. The use of only a single (heavy) jousting *tasset* is also notable, being a distinctive feature of Italian and West European jousting armours; sometimes the German interpretation of this form included a smaller right tasset.

◄ The Hürnheim garniture configured for the Welsches Rennen. © The Wallace Collection, London

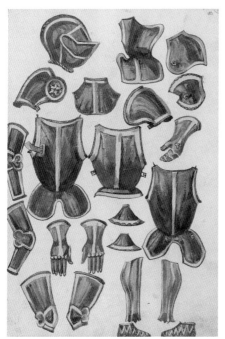

▲ Armour for the Welsches Rennen ('foreign joust of war'), from an armour album, Augsburg, *c*.1560–70. © The J. Paul Getty Museum, Los Angeles

This armour is essentially the same as that used in the *Welsches Gestech*, the main difference being the smooth, body-formed grandguard and lack of a tilt. Earlier in the sixteenth century the *Welsches Rennen* was run with single-pointed lances, but here coronels are clearly shown.

The equipment for the second of the latest German jousting fashions in vogue during the mid sixteenth century, the *Neue Welsches Gestech*, was very similar to that for the new foreign joust of war, except that the grandguard remained more shield-like in its shape (although it was also moulded to the shoulder at the top) and usually had a raised lattice of bars or thick ridges to catch the lance in order to prevent the opponent's lance from skating (see also p. 70). This form was also of course run with a tilt.

▲ Visor and reinforcing bevor for the 'new foreign joust over the tilt', from the 'Kings' garniture of the future Emperor Maximilian II, made by Matthäus Frauenpreiss the Elder and etched by Jörg Sorg, Augsburg, dated 1549. IV.423, III.1071

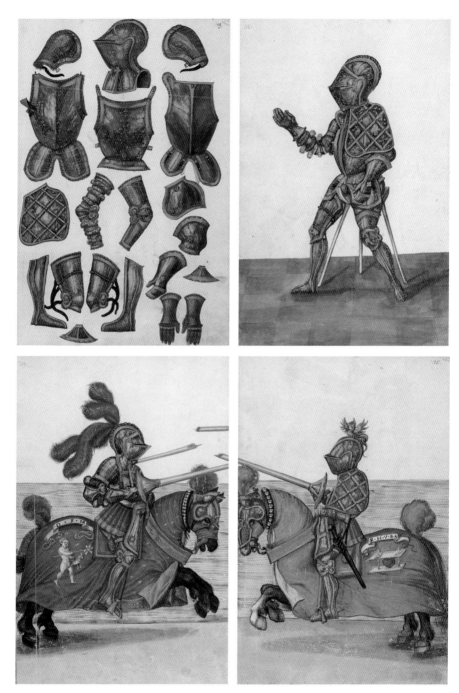

▲ The armour for the Welsches Gestech ('Foreign joust of peace'), from an armour album, Augsburg, *c.*1560–70. Here armour closely similar to the equipment for the Welsches Rennen is used at the tilt, which the artist has decided to place behind both jousters for the sake of technical clarity. © The J. Paul Getty Museum, Los Angeles

THE GERMAN JOUST OF
WAR AND THE FREE TOURNEY

The fact that the chevron garniture originally had another set of jousting pieces is revealed by the survival of the additional manifer, a defence for the left hand quite different from the reinforce for the 'foreign' jousts. This piece is more closely fitted to the forearm, with a narrower cuff, and with the plates covering the digits shaped to resemble the individual finger assemblies of a field gauntlet. It was required for German jousts of war and the 'free tourney', a battle-like mêlée which began with a lance charge and continued as a mounted sword fight. Free tourneys were sometimes preceded by individual jousts using the same equipment. Here the reinforcing pieces, which were not part of a basic war armour, were shaped so that they looked less different from the armour worn on the battlefield, from a distance at least. The grandguard was designed to look more like a typical field pauldron, usually with a vertical haute-piece providing additional protection to the neck, which was itself more lightly guarded by a wrapper that permitted the head to turn (which the 'foreign' reinforcing bevor did not). The embossed fingers on the second manifer of the chevron garniture were then meant to make this heavy jousting piece look superficially like a lighter field gauntlet.

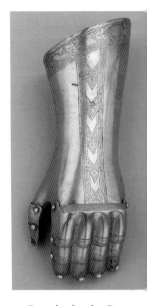

▲ Gauntlet for the German Joust of War and Free Tourney, from the Hürnhein garniture, Augsburg, c.1540
© The Wallace Collection, London

▲ The armour for the Freiturnier ('Free Tourney'), from an armour album, Augsburg, c.1560–70. This versi of the free tourney armour appears to incorporate standard field gauntlets rather than specialised armour for one or both hands. However it is clear that dedicated tournament gauntlets were sometimes worn in this typ of contest, which began with a lance charge (the lances here, already broken, carry coronels) and continued a a combat with swords. © The J. Paul Getty Museum, Los Angeles

THE DECLINE OF THE JOUST OF WAR

In his *Doctrine of the Art of Chivalry* (1548), the Castilian knight and jouster Juan Quijada de Reayo explains the exchange pieces for the joust, before arguing that they are useless, expressing his preference for jousting in field armour:

These harnesses … reinforced with iron are very gamely, but they have been of no benefit to the knights I have seen who have jousted in them, for in my time I have seen many men killed by blows to the visor …

… I never jousted with a reinforced harness because I have always been comfortable with the Castilian style of harness.

Quijada posits that if the same fundamental danger exists regardless of whether one wears jousting armour or field harness, one might as well choose the lighter, more comfortable war gear; the threat persists regardless. He distinguishes between his 'Castilian' armour and reinforced jousting armour, so it must have been a form of field armour, perhaps with subtler reinforces like armour for the free tourney.

Quijada was not the only one who had felt this way. Jousts in field armour with minimal or no reinforcement remained widespread up to c. 1550. Even at the most cordial court festivals, jousts in war armour still had a place, most notably at the great chivalric spectacle held in the presence of the Emperor Charles V at Binche in 1549. With his son Prince Philip participating as the leading combatant, all jousts at Binche were still run in field harness, facilitating a large number of participants. In fact none of the equestrian combats required special armour, and thus over sixty knights fought in the pas d'armes, jousts and free tourney over several days. There were numerous injuries, but luckily no deaths.

Nevertheless, and despite all the advantages enjoyed when running in field harness, jousts of war appear to have begun a decline after *c.*1550. The fact was that war armour, being lighter and more flexible, was also vulnerable to repeated attacks with the couched lance. On the battlefield, it might only need to save the wearer's life at one crucial moment in the charge, but in the lists, the armour was struck again and again. Jousting armour was designed to withstand that single repeated threat, but field harness was not. The risk of equipment failure was greater.

While visiting Augburg in the company of Prince Philip of Spain some months after the Binche spectacle, Don Garcia de Toledo, Marqués de Villafranca, ordered an elaborate garniture from the armourer Anton Peffenhauser. Including an extensive array of exchange pieces, this garniture was comprised of three complete armours, each of which could be worn in a number of different configurations. Along with field and tournament applications, this armour provided pieces for all forms of joust then practiced at the Spanish–Burgundian and Austrian Habsburg courts. While many of the elements have been lost, a significant portion of the jousting armour is now in the Royal Armouries,

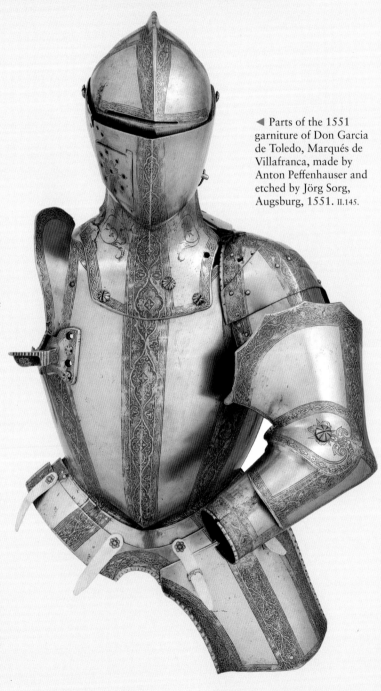

◀ Parts of the 1551 garniture of Don Garcia de Toledo, Marqués de Villafranca, made by Anton Peffenhauser and etched by Jörg Sorg, Augsburg, 1551. II.145.

and other parts are found in the Wallace Collection and the Metropolitan Museum of Art. The helmet grimly expresses an awareness of the dreadful risk of penetration of the eyes, with a sight almost entirely blocked off on the left side – the primary striking zone. Perhaps the Marqués had seen other noblemen struck through the skull and killed. His contemporary Juan Quijada certainly did, as he states in his *Doctrine*:

> *I have seen many men killed by blows through the visor. First, the son of the Count of Oñate, at the Queen's Palace; Don Luis Osorio, at Tafalla in Navarre; and in Saragossa, Don Gaspar, son of the Count of Sástago; and Hieronymus Dansa. I have seen all of these men die after being hit, as well as others whose names I shall not mention.*

◀ Reinforcing bevor and gardbrace (grandguard) for the jousts in the Italian style, from the 1551 garniture of Don Garcia de Toledo. © The Wallace Collection, London

▲ The 1551 garniture of Don Garcia de Toledo, as recorded in the album of the etcher Jörg Sorg, Augsburg, 1548–63. © Wurtembergische Landesbibliothek, Stuttgart

▲ The fatal wounding of King Henri II of France, from the series of prints made for *Histoires diverses qui sont mémorables touchant les guerres, massacres et troubles, advenues en France en ces dernières années* by Jean Perrissin and Jacques Tortorel of Lyons, printed in Geneva, 1570. © British Museum

The looming dangers of the joust became impossible to ignore on 30 June 1559, when King Henri II of France, successor of Francis I, was mortally wounded in a joust. Ironically, the event was a celebration of the Treaty of Cateau-Cambrésis, which had finally brought an end to the Italian Wars which had raged since the 1490s and which the Field of Cloth of Gold had failed to stop. In what can only have been a terrible accident, the French king's helmet was penetrated by a fragment of his opponent's lance, which had struck accurately on the left shoulder and broken. A sharp piece of the shattered lance continued upwards, penetrating the sight of the king's visor and transfixing his head from left eye to right ear. The King's death cannot be attributed to equipment failure, human error or ill-intent; it was just very bad luck.

▶ King Henri II of France, by Léonard Limosin, *c.*1555–60.
© Metropolitan Museum of Art, New York

▶ Portrait medal of Catherine de Medici, Queen of King Henri II, dressed as a widow, with a broken lance on the reverse with the inscription LACRIMÆ • HINC • HINC • DOLOR • ('Tears from this, from this sorrow'), French, *c.*1600. © British Museum

JOUSTING IN THE LATER SIXTEENTH CENTURY

The old style of *Stechen* or German joust of peace (run in heavy armour incorporating a large *Stechhelm*) continued to be run into the second half of the sixteenth century, albeit for the most part only by the German middle classes. The most notable event was the civic jousting festival or *Gesellenstechen* ('Bachelors' joust') held annually in the city of Nuremburg up to 1561. Among the high nobility it had fallen out of fashion by *c*.1550 at the absolute latest, and probably earlier in many parts of the Empire. At the same time, true, undiluted jousts of war were becoming less common due to the higher level of risk, although they did remain a feature of Habsburg courtly spectacles into the 1560s. Still, other joust forms continued to flourish, varying from place to place and from event to event. In the second half of the sixteenth century, various types of course at the tilt dominated, while jousts in the open field or 'at random' steadily dwindled.

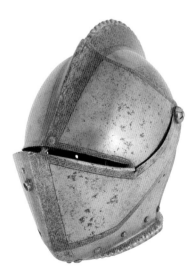

◀▼ Close-helmet for the joust, Augsburg, *c*.1560. IV.572

◀ Detail of jousts of war run in the open field, part of a military spectacle held in Vienna in June 1560, from *The Tournament Book of Knightly Acts*, illustrated by Hanns Lautensack, 1561. © Metropolitan Museum of Art, New York

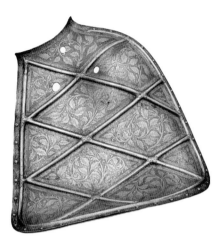

▲ Shield for the Welsches Gestech, from the 'Rose-leaf' garniture of Emperor Maximilian II, made by Franz Grosschedel, Landshut, 1571. III.87

▲ Detail of a jouster armed for the Welsch Gestech, from the Tournament Book of Arc Ferdinand II of Tyrol, c.1557. © KHM, Vienna

From the middle of the sixteenth century, two main styles of jousting armour were used for running at the tilt in Germany. Both courses were often referred to as 'foreign' jousts, because of the use of the tilt, although they were different in design. The first is most easily recognised by its distinctive steel shield, shaped to the left shoulder at the top but swept out and away from the body at the bottom like the wooden jousting shields of former times; like them, this plate was known as the *Stechtartsche* in German. However, instead of being strapped in place, this shield was bolted onto the neck and shoulder, and often criss-crossed with a lattice formed of raised ridges. These ridges ensured that good lance-breaks took place by preventing the spearhead from slipping off the metal surface. Assisting the opponent's lance to gain purchase might seem counter-intuitive, but it was in fact an important safety measure. A skating lance could travel dangerously up into the neck or face, downwards into the groin, or sideways into the right shoulder, and no opponent, however well-meaning, could stop it. Interestingly, earlier latticed shields usually had ridges formed of applied steel bars riveted in

▲ Joust at the marriage of Alessandro Far Duke of Parma and Infanta Maria of Portu (Brussels, 11 November, 1565).
© University of Warsaw Library

place, while later examples have embossed ridges. This suggests that the applied ridges were vulnerable to being bent and even torn off when struck. In versions of the game where a higher level of difficulty was desired, the latticework was omitted, making it harder to land a good blow.

Courses run in genuinely foreign (especially Italian) jousting armour, or German armour which more accurately emulated it, had always been more challenging for the same reason, since they involved grandguards which were moulded to the left shoulder, sculpted to the form of the whole left side of the torso and polished perfectly smooth. In the later sixteenth century the German versions of this style achieved closely similar performance characteristics to, for example, actual Italian armours, albeit through slightly different means. The feet were protected with integral sabatons, rather than the boot stirrups preferred in Italy. Also the 'foreign' armour worn in German jousts was much more gracefully formed to the head and neck, while authentic Italian armour of the later sixteenth century was characterised by a very deep, angular bevor, the medial keel of which dropped in a strong, straight line down to the sternum. This created a distinctively abstract form which masked rather than flattered the form of the human being inside.

▲ Armour for the Welsches Gestech, made by Anton Peffenhauser, Augsburg, c.1580.
© The Wallace Collection, London

JOUSTING ARMOUR FROM THE ELECTORAL COURT OF SAXONY, *c.1580–1610*

Beyond the Imperial court, distinct jousting traditions flourished elsewhere in Germany too. During the sixteenth and seventeenth centuries, the Electors of Saxony maintained their own vibrant jousting culture. Jousts were held annually at their court in Dresden, to celebrate the end of Lent, and to mark christenings, marriages, and diplomatic missions. Of the several joust forms popular in Saxony, certain variations of the Rennen are most closely associated with the Electors and their circle. Several armour styles can now be identified as distinctively Saxon, their design derived from the true Rennen armours of the time of Maximilian I. The Royal Armouries possesses two Saxon jousting armours, one dating from the late sixteenth century and the other from the early seventeenth, and both involving an intriguing combination of Rennen and Stechen elements.

The helmets are heavy sallets, worn with a thick defence for the lower face secured with a large bolt and wing-nut positioned in front of the nose. The later armour also includes a thick metal bracket connecting the rear of the helmet to the backplate, to prevent the head from being thrown back when struck. On the earlier armour, Rennen features are combined with defences for the left shoulder and arm normally associated with the Welsches Gestech or 'foreign' joust at the tilt. The swept shield preserved on this armour was originally worn with a small reinforce bolted to the left couter (now lost). These defences are essentially the same as those on late Stechen armours of the more typical Augsburg style. This is not surprising, since this armour was made in Augsburg, for use in Dresden. The plates for the left shoulder are different on the later example, which is part of a series of early seventeenth-century armours for the Pallien Rennen (run at the tilt, or *Pallia*). These armours were actually made in Dresden, not in Augsburg. The Saxon Electors of this time were enthusiastic followers of Italian fashion, and this Dresden-made armour reveals a strong Italian influence. The grandguard is shaped to the top of the shoulder and also, like its Italian counterparts, to the left side of the chest, with a large, wing-like pasguard.

While they do preserve some of the spirit of the true Rennen, these armours were in fact worn in jousts run at the tilt with light, frangible lances; the risks embraced by past generations were clearly no longer acceptable.

▲ Armour for the Pallien Rennen, German (Saxon), *c.*1600. II.170

◄ Armour for the Pallien Rennen, made in Augsburg for the Saxon court, *c.*1580–90. II.185

John the Steadfast, Elector of Saxony (1467–1532, Elector from 1525) is known to have competed in 125 jousts and tournaments between 1487 and 1527. These combats included Rennen and Stechen on at least twenty-two occasions. In 1498 he encountered the Emperor Maximilian himself in the Gestech, and lost. In 1502 he ran against his predecessor the Saxon Elector Fredrik the Wise (1463–1525, Elector from 1486) in a Rennen held at Torgau in northwest Saxony.

John Fredrik the Magnanimous (1503–1554, Elector from 1532) was perhaps the greatest of the Saxon jousting champions, competing in ninety-nine Stechen, thirty-eight Rennen, one joust in the 'foreign' fashion, and eight *Halbierungen*, in which one jouster was equipped in Rennen armour and armed with a multi-pronged lance for the Gestech, while his opponent wore Stechen armour and carried a single-pointed Rennen lance.

Augustus (1526–1586, Elector from 1553) was the last of the Saxon Electors to practice the true Rennen. Between 1543 and 1566 he participated in fifty-five Rennen, including two Halbierungen. He clearly was an extremely talented jouster: in 1566 he welcomed his good friend the Archduke Ferdinand of Tyrol (son of the Emperor Ferdinand I) to Dresden, where they competed against each other in the Rennen. Ferdinand was quickly unhorsed. Augustus also won the

▲ John I 'the Steadfast' Duke and Elector of Saxony, by Lucas Cranach, 1532–3. © Metropolitan Museum of Art, New York

▲ John Fredrik I 'the Magnanimous', Duke and Elector of Saxony, German, c.1550. © Metropolitan Museum of Art, New York

jousts celebrating the coronation of King Fredrik II of Denmark (1559). A great aficionado, he is known to have lent jousting armour, horses, and armourers to other noblemen, indicating that he maintained a sporting armoury of unusual size and quality.

By the end of the sixteenth century jousting was becoming less fashionable, and the wider decline extended even to the Saxon court. Augustus' son Christian I (1560–91) was a keen horseman and installed a tiltyard at his palace at Dresden, but it is clear that he only ever intended to use it for the tamer pastime of running at the ring. The age of the jousting Electors was over.

▲ Sallet and reinforcing bevor for the Pallien Rennen, German (Saxon), *c.*1600.
© The Wallace Collection, London

LATE JOUSTING HELMETS, *c.*1580–1620

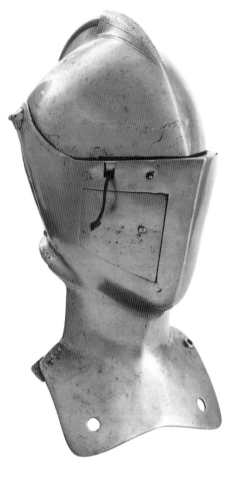

By the middle of the sixteenth century the close-helmet had superseded the old 'frog-mouthed' helm as the most common form of head defence used in most jousts. Fashion throughout the mid- to late 1500s, and indeed into the 1600s, required jousting armour to be more flattering and finely sculpted to the wearer's physique. The bulkier aesthetic popular in the late fifteenth and early sixteenth centuries had steadily faded away. The newer head defences needed to provide the same level of protection as the helm, but now also had to be much more closely-fitted. The close-helmet achieved this form-fitting shape by utilising a bevor or chin-defence that pivoted up and down on the same points as the visor. Thus the whole front of the helmet could be opened to accept the head, then closed and locked

▲ Close-helmet for the joust, North Italian, *c.*1580. IV.39

◀ Close-helmet for the joust, Augsburg, *c.*1590. IV.414

down around it. Like their predecessors, close-helmets for the joust were built very strongly, with the thick metal lined with densely-padded textile. Also, the helmet was usually held in suspension over the top of the wearer's skull by means of special cross-straps attached to the inside of the helmet with adjustable laces.

Once again, form and function went hand in hand. It is notable that both attributes are addressed together by the Castilian knight Luis Zapata de Chaves in his 1589 work *On The Jouster*, a treatise on horsemanship and mounted combat. Describing the key requirements of a good close-helmet for the joust, Zapata recommends that

The close-helmet should not be too pointed, for this looks like a rooster; nor too unsightly or too blunt, for this looks like an owl; rather, it should be handsomely proportioned and sized, with padding on the inside, so that the blows do not resound, your head bridled by folding a piece of the same taffeta or silk padding and securing it to your forehead with two straps, your head pressed towards the back of the helmet so that in the erratic movements of the encounter your face does not strike the helmet. The visor must be secure and small, and fitted close to your eyes, so that you can see everything when you look through it, and may God protect you from the danger of a splinter entering your visor, for if this should ever happen, it goes without saying that it only needs to penetrate about one digit in order to be fatal.

◄ Close-helmet for the joust, Augsburg, *c.*1590. IV.415

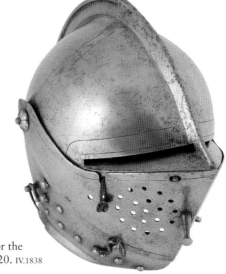

► Close-helmet for the joust, Dutch, c.1620. IV.1838

JOUSTS IN THE AGE OF ELIZABETH I

After Henry VIII's death in 1547, jousting in Tudor England went into decline. A royal joust was organised to mark the coronation of the Henry's ten year-old son King Edward VI, but after that only one major joust was held per year during his short reign, a low frequency which continued through the even shorter rule of his successor Queen Mary I (1553–8). Neither of these monarchs could participate in jousts themselves, although Edward was known to have enjoyed running at the ring. It had not ceased to exist, but the joust in England had lost much of its Henrician prestige. Jousts under Edward and Mary were no doubt colourful occasions, but they were no longer compelling socio-political statements. However, the English joust was not dead, and would enjoy one last great period.

During the forty-five year reign of Henry VIII's daughter Elizabeth I, the joust regained and indeed exceeded its former esteem, as an expression of the monarch's power, the devotion of her knights and lords, and the love of her common subjects. When it became clear later in her reign that Elizabeth would never marry, she became the focus of almost religious devotion as 'the Virgin Queen', the saviour of her people, a sacred symbol of England itself. Sometime in the 1570s, her accession to the throne began to be celebrated with a magnificent annual joust at Whitehall. During this yearly public spectacle, the noblemen of Elizabeth's court jousted in her honour, dressed in highly decorated armour and representing allegorical concepts, themes, or characters. The lists became England in microcosm, with the Queen at its heart, surrounded by her faithful knights and ladies. They in turn were encircled by a cheering audience of the Queen's common subjects packed into double-tiered viewing stands.

Since Elizabeth, as a woman, could not ride in the lists herself, she was represented by a champion. The famous knight Sir Henry Lee served as Queen's Champion from 1570 until 1590. At that point his advanced age at last forced him to retire from the honour of serving on the field as the Queen's martial surrogate. One of the greatest jousters of his generation, it had been Sir Henry's idea to celebrate the Queen's Accession Day (17 November) with a lavish annual joust. As well as Queen's Champion, Master of the Armouries, and Master of Ordinance, Sir Henry was also President of an organisation called 'The Society of Knights Tilter', apparently an Elizabethan jousting fraternity. Some of his actual jousting scores survive, and they testify to his skill. The jousting cheque for the May Day jousts of 1570 (now in the Bodleian

Library, Oxford) records that, in a typical round, Sir Henry broke five lances in six courses against Sir Edward Herbert, while another cheque, from the Accession Day joust of 1584, tells us that Sir Henry (who was then, at fifty-one, much older than most of his opponents) broke six lances in six courses run against Sir Philip Sydney.

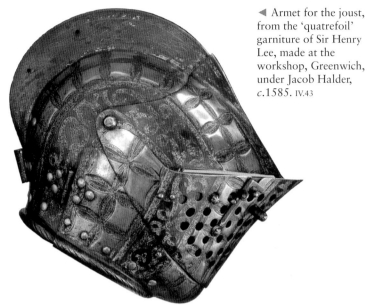

◀ Armet for the joust, from the 'quatrefoil' garniture of Sir Henry Lee, made at the workshop, Greenwich, under Jacob Halder, c.1585. IV.43

The joust at Whitehall held on 15 May 1581 is particularly well-documented, and gives a vivid picture of what

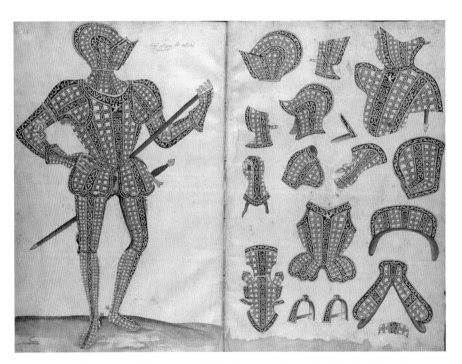

▲ Design for the 'quatrefoil' garniture of Sir Henry Lee, from the 'Almain Album', Greenwich, c.1585. © V&A Museum

▲ The three elements of an Elizabethan courtly spectacle – joust, tourney and barriers, by William Smith, Rouge Dragon Persuivant, College of Arms, 1597. © Acton Achieves

an Elizabethan joust was like. The event was held to welcome French ambassadors who were trying to arrange a marriage between the Queen and Hercule François, Duke of Anjou and Alençon. The tenans, Sir Philip Howard, Earl of Arundel, Frederick, 4th Baron Windsor, Sir Philip Sydney, and Sir Fulke Grenville, assumed the allegorical role of 'The Four Foster Children of Desire'. The Queen's viewing gallery, at the north end of the Whitehall tiltyard (to give the Queen the perfect view, straight down the line of the tilt), was transformed into 'The Fortress of Perfect Beauty'. The four tenans appeared in richly etched and gilt armour, and before the combats commenced, each

▲ George Clifford, 3rd Earl of Cumberland, by Nicholas Hilliard, English, c.1590. © Royal Museums Greenwich

delivered a lengthy poem, flowery address, or witty speech to the Queen. They then defended the 'Golden Fleece' against twenty-one venans, two of whom, Sir Thomas Parrot and Anthony Cooke, appeared as Adam and Eve, with the latter's helmet covered with long, cascading hair. Interestingly, Sir Henry Lee made a sudden, intentionally mysterious appearance as an 'Unknown Knight', breaking six lances against his opponent before immediately disappearing out of the tiltyard gates. All those involved in this extraordinary display fought hard to impress their Queen, and the day's jousting and tourney combat was described as 'very strenuous'.

AN ARMOUR OF THE EARL OF LEICESTER

During the reign of Henry VIII it had been somewhat unusual (but by no means unknown) for the Greenwich royal workshop to make armour for anyone other than the king. After his death, however, select noblemen were allowed buy special warrants to have armour made by the royal armourers. Under Elizabeth, Greenwich garnitures became badges of special royal favour, possessed only by her most trusted advisors and supporters. In these conditions, Greenwich work became more individualised and elaborate than ever before.

One of the most spectacular Greenwich armours in the Royal Armouries is that of Queen Elizabeth's favourite Robert Dudley, Earl of Leicester. It was made in about 1575, possibly for the Queen's three-week visit to Dudley's castle at Kenilworth in Warwickshire, during which time he entertained her with fantastical pageants, equestrian displays, and banquets. The armour now retains only its pieces of exchange for the joust, and it is impossible to know the full original extent of the garniture.

▲ Garniture of Sir Robert Dudley, Earl of Leicester, by John Kelte, Greenwich, c.1575. II.81

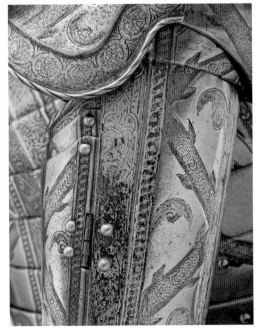

▲ Details of the garniture of Sir Robert Dudley, Earl of Leicester, by John Kelte, Greenwich, c.1575. II.81

It may have included pieces for the field and tourney, but if it did, they do not survive. In its present condition it remains one of the foremost exemplars of the Elizabethan jousting armour. The armet is fitted with a sturdy jousting visor, which sweeps gracefully and prow-like up to a sharp point between the eyes. Circular breaths have been punched into the right side of the visor, a standard feature. The grandguard with integral reinforcing bevor covers all of the left side of the upper body and most of the right, where it is flanged outward to protect the right shoulder from deflected lance-points. Typical Greenwich features include the hasp locking the bevor to the left side of the armet and the narrow articulating lame at the base of the left shoulder. The large pasguard, fixed to the couter of the vambrace by means of a pierced stud and pin, has been extended to generously overlap the lower edge of the grandguard, while the cuff of the heavy manifer overlaps its lower edge in turn, to thoroughly protect the entire left side of the body with several layers of hardened and tempered steel.

The Earl of Leicester's armour is also one of the most elaborately decorated of all Greenwich garnitures. The eye is immediately drawn to the sunken strapwork bands, one of the key elements of the Greenwich ornamental vocabulary. The bands are filled with very fine etched designs depicting allegorical figures, masks, trophies of arms, foliage, twisting arabesques, equestrian figures, and personal badges. These devices enhance the highly personal and individual nature of the armour, representing the owners membership of the English royal Order of the Garter and the French royal Order of St. Michael. A final layer of personalisation is provided by the inclusion of the Earl's initials 'RD' and six repetitions of the Warwick device of the bear and ragged staff (the earldom of Warwick rested with the Dudley family throughout the sixteenth century). Ragged staffs are also sunken and etched into the main surfaces of the armour between the bands, interspersed with scrolled leaves and charged with small crescents. The crescent is a heraldic *brisure* denoting a younger son, and in this case it differentiates the staff used by Robert Dudley from that employed by his older brother Ambrose, 3rd Earl of Warwick.

Despite its superb decoration, this armour today looks quite different than it did when the Earl wore it. Originally, it was brightly coloured; all of the strapwork and other etched decoration was fire-gilded, while the smooth main surfaces were heat-tinted so that they took on an iridescent blue, dark red or even purple hue. In its original condition this armour combined pictorial (etched) and three-dimensional (sunken) ornamentation with rich colours to create a unique work of art expressing the owner's titles, identity and prestige.

THE SAFETY ISSUE

Elizabethan jousts were glamorous, thrilling displays of martial and intellectual prowess which combined genuine combat on horseback with ingenious, esoteric and often enigmatic themes, symbols and references. The combats themselves were impressive and intense. At the same time however, concerted efforts to guarantee the complete safety of the participants were being made. Elizabethan jousters seem not to have been willing to take the same sort of risks that previous generations had just accepted as part of the game, and they implemented a range of measures to increase safety and reduce risk. First and most importantly, late Greenwich jousting armour offered an exceptional level of protection. The plates were fitted together and overlapped so well that no chinks were offered to the oncoming lance, while the sights of the helmets are usually as narrow as they can possibly be without completely blocking the wearer's field of vision. Secondly, it appears that the lances used in the jousts of Elizabeth's reign were quite narrow. This narrowness is indicated by a number of extant Elizabethan vamplates,

▶ Vamplate for the joust, from a lost garniture of Sir Christopher Hatton, by Jacob Halder, Greenwich, c.1585. III.890

which are designed to fit around the thickest part of the lance, just above the handgrip. Most examples have a lance aperture of only around 7 cm in diameter; the lance would then have tapered down to perhaps 3–4 cm by its midpoint, with its thickness reducing still further, if more gently, down the foremost 150 cm of its length. Such slender lances would have shattered with relative ease, giving a respectable blow but never one hard enough to unseat and potentially humiliate the mannered Elizabethan courtiers. Finally, it appears that the target area was restricted to the upper torso; aiming at the head seems to have been disallowed. Elizabethan jousting cheques only ever record lances broken on the body, unlike those of Henry VIII's time, which also register attaints to the body as well as both breaks and attaints struck on the head. The lack of attaints in the scores may indicate that the lances broke easily enough for good attaints to become irrelevant. With the adoption of fine, light lances that were easy to break, attaints may simply not have occurred often enough to be meaningful, since any decent hit would result in a break. Alternatively the scoring requirements may have been simplified so that it was easier for the audience to follow the action – the jouster had to break his lance to score.

Simplified scoring should not necessarily be taken as evidence of some kind of deterioration in the skill levels of Elizabethan jousters. The Queen's knights were without question superlative horsemen and martial artists, and many of them, men like Sir Henry Lee and Sir Robert Dudley, were jousters of advanced ability. They were just playing it safe. Serious injuries, which could ruin an important festive occasion, simply could not be allowed to occur. The Elizabethan effort to prevent accidents was very successful: not one significant jousting injury was suffered during Elizabeth's 45 years on the throne.

Cheual de Jouste

VICTORVM FEROQVA

CLARESCERE

STUART JOUSTS AND THE FINAL DECLINE

After Elizabeth died in 1603, King James I continued the tradition of the annual Accession Day festival, and two to three other major jousts were held every year for most of his reign. However it is clear that the King's heart was not in it. James himself never took part, and the lack of royal enthusiasm led personal feats of arms to lose their prominence in the courtly consciousness. Gradually King James abandoned the great popular spectacles of his predecessor's time, preferring much more exclusive, 'courtiers-only' masques and entertainments. Many of these events were conceived by the dramatist Ben Jonson, who flatly rejected the Arthurian themes and chivalric culture which had dominated for so long. The Whitehall tiltyard lost its pivotal function as the place where the connection between the monarch and the people was celebrated. King James hated crowds, preferring to glorify himself indoors. Jonson and his collaborator, the architect and stage designer Inigo Jones, probably felt that their set-pieces and drama should take precedence over any actual fighting, which undoubtedly seemed old-fashioned and irrelevant to them. Themes of responsible, educated government, and profitable trade, industry and agriculture began to be prioritised over the chivalric heroism of former days. As Jonson wrote for one Jacobean event:

But here are other acts; another stage
And scene appears; it is not since as then:
No giants, dwarfs or monsters here, but men.
His arts must be to govern and give laws
To peace no less than arms.

For a brief time it looked as though chivalry in England was about to experience a reinvigoration, in the person of the king's heir, Henry, Prince of Wales (1594–1612). The prince gave all indications of being destined to become a great knight-king. From a young age, like Prince Henry Tudor before him, Henry Stuart rode well, hunted, and was a promising martial artist. By the age of eight or even younger, Prince Henry was receiving

◄ A jousting horse led in the funeral procession of Archduke Albert 'the Pious' of Austria (d.1621), from 'Pompa Funebris ... Alberti Pii', after Jacques Francquart, 1623.
© Metropolitan Museum of Art, New York

armours as gifts, most famously from the elderly Sir Henry Lee, who gave him one of the last richly decorated armours ever produced at Greenwich, the blue and gold garniture for war, joust, and tournament made *c*.1608, now in the Royal Collection. When he received it, at the age of thirteen or fourteen, Henry was probably already the owner of at least one other jousting armour, a French one probably given to him by King Henri IV of France, whom he thanked for it in a letter dated 21 July 1607. Henry's potential as a ruler was sadly never tested; he died of typhoid fever, aged only eighteen.

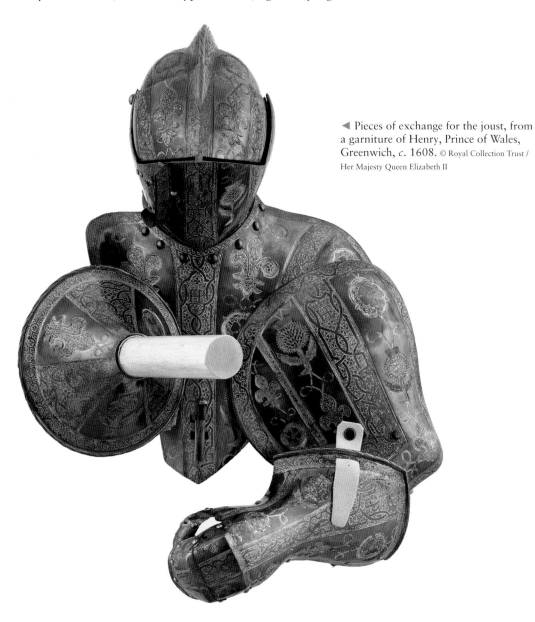

◀ Pieces of exchange for the joust, from a garniture of Henry, Prince of Wales, Greenwich, *c.* 1608. © Royal Collection Trust / Her Majesty Queen Elizabeth II

▲ Henry, Prince of Wales, by Robert Peake the elder, *c*.1606–8. © Parham House, Pulborough, West Sussex

By the end of James' reign, jousts had become rare. Finally even the Accession Day joust was postponed and then cancelled. The last royal joust to take place in England was probably held in February 1626, to celebrate the coronation and marriage of King Charles I, James' second son. By this time jousting had become so stylised and non-violent that it ceased to be meaningful as a knightly exercise, and was absorbed into the new fashion for high-school riding displays or *carousels*. One of the last published works to deal with jousting, *Le Manège Royal, L'Instruction du Roy, en L'Exercice de Monter a Cheval* ('The Royal Riding School, The Instruction of the King in Horseback Riding Exercises', published in 1623) was written by Antoine de Pluvinel, riding master to King Louis

◀ Jousting armour of Henry, Prince of Wales, French, *c*.1607. © Royal Collection Trust / Her Majesty Queen Elizabeth II

XIII of France. It presents the reader with a joust in which the safety measures employed earlier by the Elizabethans are taken to their furthest extremes. The work's beautifully-engraved plates show the armours as heavily reinforced and thoroughly protective, the same French style of jousting armour in fact as that sent to the Prince of Wales by the French king sixteen years earlier. In contrast, the lances are so narrow as to be no threat at all, constructed of an elaborately-sculpted stock of around five feet in length, into which is socketed an extremely slim end of perhaps three feet. The upper third of this weapon is so narrow that it appears no thicker than a fishing rod. Finally the rider's whole body seems to be off-limits as a target, the object of the exercise being to dislodge the opponent's *panache* of brightly-coloured ostrich and egret feathers.

▲ Detail from *Le Manège Royal, L'Instruction du Roy, en L'Exercice de Monter a Cheval* by Antoine de Pluvinel, 1623.

EPILOGUE

Throughout its five hundred year history, the joust had flourished as a physical expression of the refined essence of chivalry. In a burst of intense action, lasting only around five seconds, the encounter in the lists proved beyond all doubt that the knight, a man chosen by God to wield special divine powers, was capable of performing superhuman feats of strength, speed and endurance. In reality it was his horse and armour that bestowed these powers, along with the advanced training and mental discipline required to use them effectively. Nevertheless, in that single instant, the moment of collision, proof seemed to be manifest on earth that everything upon which society was based was altogether true: the undeniable personal power of the devout, aristocratic warrior. Jousting throughout the whole of the Renaissance emitted a profound contemporary resonance.

The history of the joust had always been inextricably intertwined with the fortune and fate of the knights themselves. As their mounted combat methods had developed, so too had the formal exercises which provided the opportunity to display those skills to the world. As weapons and armour evolved, the joust changed and diversified to maintain the best possible platform for their exhibition in action.

However, from the seventeenth century the world of the knight in Europe began to reject the basis of his existence. The personal prowess and military strength of individuals was increasingly viewed with suspicion, and was suppressed rather than celebrated. Noblemen who were trained to fight and kill from childhood, with the means to field personal armies, came to be seen as dangerous threat, not an essential asset. Although King Louis XIV of France professed esteem for the ideals of chivalry, and often portrayed himself as an equestrian hero in both performance and representational art – in horse ballets, plays and portraiture – he pulled the teeth of his nobility, removing them physically from their lands and supporters and forcing them to live with him, their absolute ruler.

Although armoured knights and gunpowder weapons had coexisted on the battlefields of Europe for over two hundred years, by the end of the sixteenth century firearms were dramatically changing the nature of warfare. Armoured cavalry had adopted firearms as a standard part of their armament as soon as it was technologically practical to do so, in the second quarter of the sixteenth century. However, it was not until the seventeenth century that the heavy cavalry lance was phased out in order to allow the armoured cavalryman, or *cuirassier* as he was now called, to carry a carbine as well as pairs of pistols. The obsolescence of the weapon at the heart of all jousts heralded the end of the exercise which had always promoted its use.

The proliferation of both field artillery and handheld firearms in the seventeenth century also made the ancient art of armoured combat on horseback difficult to maintain. A knight's warhorse was not only an expensive breed, it was also the product of years of advanced and continual training. Horses had always been lost in battle, and indeed in jousts and tournaments, but the death rates were rarely so high as to outstrip those of breeding and training. However, on the battlefields of the seventeenth century, thousands of horses could be killed in an afternoon, under the hail of gunfire and artillery bombardment. In his *Military Instructions for the Cavalry* (1632), John Cruso observed that one reason the lancer was disappearing was the lack of good horses capable of bearing a heavily armed man, while General George Monck, Duke of Albemarle, in *Observations Upon Military and Political Affairs* (written in 1644, published in 1671) noted that

I have omitted here to speak anything of the Armour of a good Cuirassier, because there are not many Countries that do afford Horses fit for the Service of Cuirassiers.

Social, political and technological factors then conspired together to spell the end of armoured knights as a military force. However as symbols in art, images of power, prestige, justice and righteousness, they endured. With the help of their armourers, the elite warriors of the Renaissance had moulded themselves into living, decorated sculptures, anthropomorphic creations who in the lists acted out perilous conflict as performance art. They made an enduring impression that has entirely outlived military usefulness. In the nineteenth century jousts were revived as a romantic reaction against an industrialised modern world which many felt was changing too fast; ancient traditions were being discarded and fundamental values lost. The remarkable Eglinton Tournament of 1839 expressed this dissatisfaction on a grand scale although, due to torrential rain on the first day and the use of unsuitable hunting and racing horses, the jousts left much to be desired.

Jousting has continued ever since. Indeed, this book is one very small result of it, the work of someone who always wanted to wear armour, ride and smite with the lance more than anything else, and who had the good fortune to join the Royal Armouries in 1996 – not as a curator, but as a jouster. But jousters were sometimes authors too, and at the end of this brief summary of an enormous and very complicated subject, the words of two of them, Juan Quijada de Reayo and the *Mossèn* Ponç de Menaguerra, both knights of King Ferdinand II of Aragon, seem most appropriate:

If I have not demonstrated the kind of intelligence required for a task such as this, I implore those who read this book to improve upon it ...

Doctrina del Arte de la Cavalleria (1548)

The remaining subtleties, left up to your lordships, shall be like diamonds that will enrich the embroidery of this poorly trimmed cloth.

Lo Cavaller (c.1493)

FURTHER READING

Anglo, S 1968 *The Great Tournament Roll of Westminster*. Oxford, Clarendon.

Anglo, S 1969 *Spectacle, Pageantry and Early Tudor Policy*. Oxford, Clarendon.

Capwell, T 2018 *Arms and Armour of the Medieval Joust*. Leeds, Royal Armouries.

Cripps-Day, F 1918 *The History of the Tournament in England and in France*. London, B. Quaritch.

Fallows, N 2010 *Jousting in Medieval and Renaissance Iberia*. Woodbridge, Boydell.

Krause, S 2019 *Freydal: The Book of Tournaments of Emperor Maximilian I*. Cologne, Taschen.

Pfaffenbichler, M (ed.) 2014 *Kaiser Maximilian I: Der Letzte Ritter und das höfische Turnier*. Regensburg, Schnell and Steiner.

Pfaffenbichler, M (ed.) 2017 *Turnier: 1000 Jahre Ritterspiele*. Vienna, Kunsthistorisches Museum.

Rangstrom, L (ed.) 1992 *Riddarlek Och Tornerspel: Tournaments and the Dream of Chivalry*, ex. cat. Stockholm, Livrustkammaren.

Terjanian, T 2019 *The Last Knight: The Art, Armor and Ambition of Maximilian I*, ex. cat. New York, Metropolitan Museum of Art.

Young, A 1987 *Tudor and Jacobean Tournaments*. London, George Philip.

ACKNOWLEDGEMENTS

This book is dedicated to Professor Noel Fallows, whose work on Medieval and Renaissance jousting treatises has much advanced our understanding of this extraordinary but oft-misunderstood subject; Plus Ultra.

I am also extremely grateful to Martyn Lawrence, Head of Publications at the Royal Armouries, for allowing me to continue the story begun in *Arms and Armour of the Medieval Joust*, to Sydney Anglo for reading and commenting on this book in draft, and to Keith Dowen of the Royal Armouries and Marina Viallon of the École pratique des hautes études, Paris for sharing their own work on the combats fought at the Field of the Cloth of Gold.

Published by Royal Armouries Museum, Armouries Drive, Leeds LS10 1LT, United Kingdom

www.royalarmouries.org

ISBN 978 0 94809 299 2

Edited by Martyn Lawrence

Designed by Riverside Publishing Solutions Limited, Salisbury, UK

Printed by Page Bros Ltd, Norwich

10 9 8 7 6 5 4 3 2

A CIP record for this book is available from the British Library

Also by Tobias Capwell: Arms and Armour of the Medieval Joust (2018)